YOU KNOW YOU LOVE ME

YOU KNOW YOU LOVE ME

How **Gossip Girl** *Changed Pop Culture as We Know It*

Lindsay Denninger

BLOOMSBURY ACADEMIC
NEW YORK • LONDON • OXFORD • NEW DELHI • SYDNEY

BLOOMSBURY ACADEMIC

Bloomsbury Publishing Inc, 1359 Broadway, 12th Floor, New York, NY 10018, USA
Bloomsbury Publishing Plc, 50 Bedford Square, London, WC1B 3DP, UK
Bloomsbury Publishing Ireland, 29 Earlsfort Terrace, Dublin, 2 D02 AY28, Ireland

BLOOMSBURY, BLOOMSBURY ACADEMIC and the Diana logo are trademarks
of Bloomsbury Publishing Plc

First published in the United States of America 2026

Copyright © Lindsay Denninger, 2026

For legal purposes the Acknowledgments on pp. 227–228 constitute an extension
of this copyright page.

Cover design: Sally Rinehart
Cover images © The CW/Photofest; © iStock.com/AndreyKrav
Back cover images © iStock.com/homydesign; © iStock.com/ksushsh;
© iStock.com/Albert_Karimov; © Stuart Gregory/Photodisc/Getty Images;
© iStock.com/Backiris; © iStock.com/Berezka_Klo

All rights reserved. No part of this publication may be: i) reproduced or transmitted in any form, electronic or mechanical, including photocopying, recording or by means of any information storage or retrieval system without prior permission in writing from the publishers; or ii) used or reproduced in any way for the training, development or operation of artificial intelligence (AI) technologies, including generative AI technologies. The rights holders expressly reserve this publication from the text and data mining exception as per Article 4(3) of the Digital Single Market Directive (EU) 2019/790.

Bloomsbury Publishing Inc does not have any control over, or responsibility for, any third-party websites referred to or in this book. All internet addresses given in this book were correct at the time of going to press. The author and publisher regret any inconvenience caused if addresses have changed or sites have ceased to exist, but can accept no responsibility for any such changes.

Library of Congress Cataloging-in-Publication Data
Names: Denninger, Lindsay author
Title: You know you love me : how Gossip Girl changed pop culture
as we know it / Lindsay Denninger.
Description: New York : Bloomsbury Academic, 2026. | Includes bibliographical references.
Identifiers: LCCN 2025039045 (print) | LCCN 2025039046 (ebook) | ISBN 9781493088096
trade paperback | ISBN 9781493088102 epub | ISBN 9798765165393 pdf
Subjects: LCSH: Gossip girl (Television program) | LCGFT: Television criticism and reviews
Classification: LCC PN1992.77.G67 D46 2026 (print) | LCC PN1992.77.G67 (ebook)
LC record available at https://lccn.loc.gov/2025039045
LC ebook record available at https://lccn.loc.gov/2025039046

ISBN:	PB:	978-1-4930-8809-6
	ePDF:	979-8-7651-6539-3
	eBook:	978-1-4930-8810-2

Typeset by Integra Software Services Pvt. Ltd.
Printed and bound in the United States of America

For product safety related questions contact productsafety@bloomsbury.com.

To find out more about our authors and books visit www.bloomsbury.com
and sign up for our newsletters.

To Henry and Sassy,
XOXO

Contents

Introduction: XOXO		1
1	ORIGINS	11
	Why the Pilot of Gossip Girl *is One of the Best Pilots of All Time*	36
2	WRITING, RECEPTION, AND RECAPS	41
	The Best and Worst Gossip Girl *Storylines*	64
3	THE FANS	71
	Gossip Girl's 11 Best Guest Stars	92
4	DIVERSITY AND DOUBLE STANDARDS	95
	The Meme that Got Us Through a Pandemic: Go Piss Girl	112
5	SEX, LIES, AND *GOSSIP GIRL*	115
	Serena Van Der Woodsen Is the Manic Pixie Dream Girl of the Upper East Side and It Sucks	133
	Gossip Girl's 7 Most Annoying Characters	138
6	THE CHUCK AND BLAIR OF IT ALL	141
	Gossip Girl's 11 Worst Romantic Pairings	156

CONTENTS

7	THE FASHION AND THE MUSIC	161
	Gossip Girl's *11 Best Music Moments*	178
	Gossip Girl's *Best Spinoff Is* NYC Prep	196
8	THE END, THE REBOOT, AND BEYOND	183
	Gossip Girl: *Where Are They Now?*	207
	Gossip Girl: *Where Are They Now: Real-Life Edition*	214

Selected References	220
Acknowledgments	227
Index	229
About the Author	245

INTRODUCTION: XOXO

Unlike Serena or Blair, I wasn't the most popular girl in school. I mean, I wasn't *unpopular*, but those "queen of the lunch table" vibes just weren't me. I had friends, but they played sports and did activities and weren't available from the hours of 3:00 p.m. and 5:30 p.m. on weekdays. Total losers, amirite? So I made new ones on my TV, which was not too far a journey from the books I absorbed myself in as a kid. My routine on school-day afternoons was as follows: get off the bus, drop everything in a pile on the floor—hopefully in my room but probably on the stair landing to give my family the right opportunity to trip on it (hi, Mom and Dad, sorry)—heat up a snack (shout-out to ham-and-cheese Hot Pockets, IYKYK), turn on the tube, and visit with my other people. You wouldn't know them. They were *older*. I was more than likely too young to be hanging out with Donna, David, Brandon, Brenda, Kelly, Dylan, and their classmates, but I was hooked on *Beverly Hills, 90210* before you could say, "Da na na na, da na na na, CLAP CLAP." I may have turned on the

TV in order to avoid algebra and calculus homework, because I got straight Cs in math no matter how hard I tried, but really, *Beverly Hills, 90210* taught this once-sheltered kid from a New York City suburb a lot about the real-world situations she and her real-world friends would encounter later on.

I watched Brenda struggle with losing her virginity. I stressed about Emily slipping Brandon that U4EA drug. (Which—was that the gateway to the Zendaya-helmed HBO teen orgy, *Euphoria?*) I saw Donna grapple with recognizing and getting out of an abusive relationship. I cried when Kelly admitted the details of her rape, even though, looking back, I have a lot of feelings about sexual abuse and assault as depicted on screen, but we'll get to that. I screamed when Dylan's dad exploded (real fans know he didn't die, but it was a shock anyway) and when Kelly got shot in the stomach and somehow developed amnesia. *Beverly Hills, 90210* had rehabs and graduations and cheating and interventions and Luke Perry (RIP, king) quoting Lord Byron. And as a teenage girl, I ate that shit up.

Of course, after watching all of *Beverly Hills, 90210* in syndication, I needed more. For me, *Beverly Hills, 90210* was like a high school romance. You think that it's the end-all, be-all, but in reality, you'll break up in your first semester of college and eventually, you'll meet someone else that's more attuned to your interests and who you are as a person, and then you'll be all "Oh, so *this* is what love is." Luckily, the 2000s were the Renaissance of teen TV, with the WB (later to become The

INTRODUCTION: XOXO

CW after combining with UPN), FOX, and more churning out shows with twenty-something actors playing high school teens. I may have ceased being a high school student in 2005, but that didn't mean I stopped following the fictional ones. I voraciously consumed basically every teen drama at the time, meaning I was playing the field with *The O.C.*, *One Tree Hill*, *Felicity*, *Dawson's Creek*, *Popular*, *Roswell*, and *Everwood*, to name a few. I was just weighing my options. Seeing what else was out there. Lots of fish in the sea and all that.

And just like that, I fell in love. True love. Let's set the scene: It was the fall of 2007 when I found myself studying abroad in London, the sole Long Islander and sole representative of my university. I picked up, traveled half a world away, and knew absolutely no one. To say I was initially homesick is an understatement. The fall of 2007 was also the time in which a little show called *Gossip Girl* debuted on The CW. I had caught the first few episodes while I was still stateside and vowed to continue my infatuation across the pond. Except the Wi-Fi at my university was so bad that it would just constantly drop (with no wired connection, thank you very much, which, don't even get me started, is this a major city in 2007 or 1960?), leaving multiple LimeWire and iTunes downloads broken over and over and over again. But I knew that I needed to see *Gossip Girl*, so my roommate and I would force our computers to download every new *Gossip Girl* episode from iTunes every week. It didn't matter how long it took. We. Would. Be. Watching.

Everyone was talking about it at home! And we couldn't be left behind for three months, lest the zeitgeist pass us by. Viewing was available only on a teeny and yet heavy Dell computer screen, but we'd pack our Oreos and milk and Cadbury Fruit & Nut bars and indulge in a little piece of the United States for an hour a week. I don't know if it was because I very much saw myself as a Serena—because I was bottle blonde and a little boho in nature and she also favored faux-suede knee-high boots like the ones I kept buying at the Primark in Piccadilly Circus (hers were Chanel, of course)—or if it was because I understood the secret New York language *Gossip Girl* spoke so much that it felt like comfort food, a salve for homesickness, to watch these pretty rich kids with pretty rich problems. *Gossip Girl* was everything I loved about the teen television of yore, with enough modern sass and New York cool to make it my absolute new obsession.

While I was soaking up every bit of the episodes, I noticed that they—both the show and the vibes—felt extraordinarily different from those of predecessors like *90210* and *Dawson's Creek*, for example, thanks to the rise of internet culture and social media. Yes, Virginia, there was a world before social media, and it was way different. Because of the wildfire word-of-mouth that came with a hot show like *Gossip Girl*, plus the powers of the fledgling internet before it became a hub for "bean soup" and misinformation, *Gossip Girl*'s cast of

INTRODUCTION: XOXO

relatively unknown actors became instantly uber-famous overnight. They were everywhere! And suddenly, it was possible to know exactly where Blair Waldorf got her headbands and tights—the now-defunct, absolutely perfect department store Henri Bendel, BTW—and then possibly get them yourself. The rapid-fire pace of social media and the internet allowed for "Hey, did you see this new show?" and "OMG, what just happened?" and "What song is playing in this scene?" and "I have to find that shirt she's wearing." Fans like me could get instant results and spark instant conversation, and for the time, this was a new frontier. *Gossip Girl* was the show that launched thousands of Tumblr pages, millions of tweets, and dozens of LiveJournal mentions from people like me. There were all kinds of fan pages and Reddits and MySpace moments dedicated strictly to the fandom of *Gossip Girl* and whatever character each fan was "stanning" at that particular moment. The music. The clothes. The attractive actors. The must-see moments. None of it would have moved so far without the wild, wild west of the 2007 internet. The only show of that time that used the internet—games and tricks and landing pages and mysteries (but no social media)—to stir its fan base up was *LOST*, and the Dharma Initiative wasn't nearly as sexy as Chace Crawford. Plus, *Gossip Girl* was *on the internet* and *about the interne*t, whereas shows like *LOST* just used online supplemental content to keep fans engaged.

(What was Serena Van Der Woodsen if not the world's very first influencer, BTW? She would have absolutely slayed selling on TikTok shop, don't you think? She would never stoop so low as to shill for powdered greens online, but I do see Serena as one of those girlies that convinces you that a red-light therapy mask and the right workout set will change your life when it's really generational wealth and good genes that make her who she is, like Lauren Santo Domingo, who I am obsessed with.)

The entire premise of *Gossip Girl* was built around an internet blogger (remember bloggers? We call them Substack writers now) who spied on the residents of the Upper East Side. While *Beverly Hills, 90210* and other teen shows of the past inspired fashion, language, and trends in the culture at large, *Gossip Girl* did it with the accelerant of social media. And though it had an early primetime viewing slot on The CW, *Gossip Girl* pushed the envelope on what could be done on a network drama in terms of sex and drugs and teenage shenanigans. Spoiler alert: it did not make friends with critics and parents. And, reader, teens and adults alike loved that!

Gossip Girl made the viral marketability of a show a thing— *Pretty Little Liars*' villain, A, could not have made it as far as they did without *Gossip Girl* first lurking in every Upper East Side corner. Shows like *Pretty Little Liars* and *Euphoria* became millennial and Gen-Z water-cooler talk (or is it just Stanley talk or something now in the 2020s?) because Serena and Blair did it

INTRODUCTION: XOXO

first. Come to think of it, *Gossip Girl* had a disappointing reveal in its series finale (Dan was Gossip Girl, which, don't worry, we will talk plenty about later) and then *Pretty Little Liars* did, too! That's called precedent, people!

And it's not like *Gossip Girl* is any less culturally significant today than it was in 2007. Why else would it have gotten a short-lived reboot on HBO Max? Why else would fans have gone feral when the show was taken off Netflix to start streaming on HBO Max only to go back to Netflix again due to popular demand and more streaming cash? A *Gossip Girl* meme even provided plenty of laughs and imagination even through the darkest days of the Covid-19 pandemic (Go Piss Girl!). Brightly colored tights and wide, prim headbands are a thing because Blair Waldorf put them in the fashion zeitgeist in the 2000s. (Well, costumer and fashion icon Eric Daman did, but we'll get to that.) Though *Gossip Girl* certainly had its problems—there's a distinct lack of diversity and fair LGBTQ+ representation, to start—it made an impact, and it continues to provide a safe place to land for both teens and adults. It's a salve for troubling times. It's comfortable. The TV equivalent of mashed potatoes and gravy.

So why the trip down memory lane? Because I, like you, reader, am now an adult with a job and responsibilities and knees that pop when she gets out of bed. Kind of a bummer, right? Sometimes, it's nice to get lost in a dramatic story *à la* our parents' soap operas. Or harken back to when the biggest decision you made in a day is where you went out to lunch during seventh period, because you definitely weren't going to French, and your older boyfriend had a car to sneak you off campus. (Not that I, uh, would know anything about that.)

The stories of *Gossip Girl* shaped my adolescent years at the point where I needed them the most, which is probably why I've watched the show over and over again instead of streaming any of the new content Netflix and Amazon make for me. I admire Josh Schwartz and Stephanie Savage more than I do the people who run countries, because at least Josh and Stephanie know they're making it up as they go along, and everyone is Hollywood

Blair Waldorf and her army of mean girls, on the precipice of taking over television.
Photo by KC Bailey/The CW Network/Photofest © The CW Network.

INTRODUCTION: XOXO

levels of cuter. If and when you have the time to binge, *Gossip Girl* is worth a first watch, a tenth watch, a 150,000th watch—and now, should you read on (you should), you'll have the scoop on how *Gossip Girl* became *Gossip Girl* and its impact on TV from the people that lived it and loved it.

You know you love it.

1

ORIGINS

TV Before *Gossip Girl*

Before we dive into the world of elite Manhattan teenagers, lazily knotted ties as necklaces, and spending Tuesday nights at your regular table at Butter, we have to understand the television landscape of the early 2000s and why *Gossip Girl* was able to make as much of a splash as it did. Wait, let's go back—we have to understand the television landscape from its inception. Time for a history lesson! (A fairly quick one, though, I promise!) The first big three US television networks were ABC, CBS, and NBC. That's right—there was no cable, no streaming, no nothing else. And you had to *actually get up to change the channels with a knob*. Truly horrifying. Anyway, these networks were originally founded in the 1920s as radio programming that served as a kind of predecessor of the television shows we see today. There were live quiz shows, talk shows, news shows, and scripted series, including Orson Welles' *War of the Worlds* (a retelling of the H.G. Wells story), which in 1938 caused nationwide panic and catastrophic newspaper headlines because so many listeners thought that aliens were actually invading planet Earth. Yes, media literacy has been an issue in the United States since the beginning.

Following World War II, technology had caught up to the average American enough that ABC, CBS, and NBC set their sights (and appetite for advertising dollars) on television programming instead of radio. More people could afford TVs, and more people were ditching their radios in favor of being able to see their stories, too. After some trial and error to determine what radio shows could carry over to TV, we began the age of the "classic" television of the 1950s and 1960s that many of us remember from watching Nick at Nite under the covers in bed—*I Love Lucy, Leave It to Beaver, Gunsmoke, Bewitched, Gilligan's Island, The Munsters, The Andy Griffith Show, My Three Sons, Green Acres*, and many more. These shows were mostly conservative or family-value driven, had rural or suburban settings, and were cast very, very white—not all that surprising in the age of the Baby Boomer and the "good old days" of post-G.I. Bill economic prosperity. But TV took on a whole new vibe as the counterculture movements of the late 1960s and 1970s shifted to the more diverse, progressive programming of Norman Lear (*All in the Family, Maude, Good Times*) and his acolytes, who wrote their shows around people of color, single women, and urban dwellers. But mostly, if you were watching TV in the back half of the twentieth century, you had few choices of channel and virtually no diversity of people and programming. It was that or—gasp—*read a book*. Again, horrifying!

Then in 1987 came the sea change. Rupert Murdoch and Barry Diller, two men who are still having an impact on media culture as I write these words, founded FOX as an alternative choice to the ho-hum big three networks. FOX sought to capture the eyeballs of the advertiser-loved 18–49 age demographic, and they largely succeeded because their programming was, for the time, so off-the-wall and different than what anyone else was doing at the time. Shows like *Married . . . With Children*, *The Simpsons*, *COPS*, *21 Jump Street*, and *The Tracey Ullman Show* were incredibly subversive versions of the "uncool" stuff that was airing on the more traditional networks. In 1990, *Sex and the City* creator Darren Star and *Charlie's Angels* creator Aaron Spelling brought *Beverly Hills, 90210* to FOX, and teenage drama history as we know it was set. Two other networks, UPN and The WB, both arrived in 1995, quickly developing shows with a focus on teenage soap operas and programming for younger and more diverse audiences. Hooray! Finally, something for the youth.

Those who didn't live through the late 1990s and early 2000s, with their limited amount of programming (we had cable but there was no streaming, and if you had to record something, you had to use a VHS tape that you hoped didn't have your parent's wedding or sister's graduation or something), missed a true golden age of teen programming and the start of the very long producing careers of Josh Schwartz, Stephanie Savage, Joss Whedon, Darren Star, Ryan Murphy, Greg Berlanti, JJ Abrams, and many more. We were all watching *The O.C., Popular, One Tree Hill, Felicity, Gilmore Girls, Buffy the Vampire Slayer, Dawson's Creek, Charmed, Smallville, Roswell,* and *Everwood*. The WB (and, FOX, if you were watching *The O.C.*, which I was) had us all in a chokehold. The TV shows felt fresh and new and relevant, and they were full of attractive people with attractive, dramatic problems, which was especially poignant if you were in high school and everything felt heightened and theatrical. There was also, if you weren't watching UPN and pretty much only UPN, a distinct lack of diversity when it came to people of color, people with disabilities, and positive LGBTQ+ stories (and don't get me started on the body shaming of the time!), but we will *definitely* get to that one later.

Another thing worth noting is that many millennials and Gen X were on Friendster (ask your parents), MySpace (ask your older siblings), and the beginnings of Facebook at the time, but there was no other social media in the way we know it today. We had the beginnings of Tumblr, but it wasn't as easy to be internet friends and share things across the globe. No way to quickly disseminate information or chat online with your friends about this amazing new show that you just saw. You could go to school and talk about *The O.C.* in homeroom or between classes, but that was pretty much it. These shows felt new and exciting and sexy and fun, but it was all pretty analog when it came to their impact.

In 2006, per *Entertainment Weekly*, ratings had gone down enough and production costs had risen enough that the powers that be decided to combine The WB and UPN into one big ol' network merger. This led to a lot of confusion, hesitance, and I'm sure frustration and anger for showrunners and creators because you had the shows of two different networks competing for spots in what was now just one network. It's not like you can program three one-hour programs into the 8:00–9:00 p.m. hour. In the end, The CW featured seven shows from The WB and six shows from UPN (including *Veronica Mars*, starring Gossip Girl herself, Kristen Bell), premiering in the fall of 2006.

It was around that same time that Dawn Ostroff, the then-head of programming for The CW, approached *O.C.* creator Josh Schwartz about developing a show around the series of *Gossip Girl* novels that had begun publishing in 2002. And the TV landscape as we knew it changed forever.

The main cast of *Gossip Girl* promoting the first season of the show.
Photo by Scott Wintrow/Getty Images.

The Beginning

Interestingly enough, the *Gossip Girl* book series did not start as a magical idea written under the cover of night but instead as intellectual property on behalf of Alloy Entertainment. Cecily von Ziegesar, who penned the series, recounted the conception to Mediabistro:

> *Gossip Girl* came out of a brainstorming meeting, and I was assigned to the project. I wrote the proposal, coming up with the characters and the plot of the first book, as well as writing the first Gossip Girl column. We sent my proposal out to a bunch of publishers and Cindy Eagan, an editor at Little Brown Children's Books, was very enthusiastic.

Von Ziegesar continued:

> When she came in for a first meeting to discuss it, she asked who'd written the proposal. I raised my hand, and she said, "Well you have to write the books." She was my champion, insisting that my name also be on the books, instead of a fake name, a method which the company tended to use in case the writer of a series changed.

Von Ziegesar wrote the first two books of the *Gossip Girl* series while she was still working her day job. As she told *Esquire*, she wasn't even sure how it was going to pan out, given the sexy subject matter:

> I was very much writing to entertain myself—to write a book that I didn't think existed yet. I really didn't think anyone was going to read it. I thought it was just going to fizzle and die on the shelf. I think that even the publisher, Little Brown, was a bit nervous about it, because it was racy and irreverent. They did a very small print run. The books didn't become bestsellers until the third book came out. They came out every six months—the first in spring 2002, then the next in fall 2002, and then when the third was about to come out in spring 2003, it was on the bestseller list before it was actually on shelves.

Of the inspiration for the stories, von Ziegesar said,

I didn't have kids yet, and being in my twenties, I still had almost the same mindset I had in high school, so it really wasn't that much of a stretch for me to be writing the books. I had no trouble remembering what it was like, because I went to a small private school for girls on the Upper East Side. I fictionalized everything, but I based the character Dan on myself, and then I created these other characters based on people that I knew, mixing their personalities and names.

As the books churned out, von Ziegesar learned that Alloy Entertainment was looking to make *Gossip Girl*, the book series, into *Gossip Girl*, the TV series. "It took over my life, but in a good way . . . My first reaction was fear. I thought, 'I hope it's good. Please make it not be terrible!' I was on set when they were filming the pilot. The cast was wonderful and it all looked really good, but I still hadn't seen the final thing," she said.

I was really, really thrilled with it. I remember writing the last few lines of the first book and thinking, "This is good." I had a similar feeling after watching the pilot of the show. It became beyond anything I ever could have imagined. I wasn't involved in the writing of the show. But it was still my characters, and they would give the books little nods that I felt like only I understood. . . . What I hope I've done well in these books is bring you inside of characters who seem totally unapproachable—people who seem to be so privileged and gorgeous and untouchable. I think I make them feel very much human.

ORIGINS

As far as putting these humans on TV, it hadn't been the first time someone had tried. "We had taken a couple of cracks at developing the *Gossip Girl* books elsewhere. There was a script at Fox, and then we took a shot at a feature," Leslie Morgenstein, CEO of Alloy Entertainment, who owns *Gossip Girl*, told *The Hollywood Reporter*. "The rights came back to us a couple months before The CW merger. We spent some time talking about how both Fox and The WB really broke through with sexy teen soaps: *90210* on Fox, *Dawson's Creek* on The WB. It seemed to us like *Gossip Girl* had the potential to be that for The CW."

Peter Roth, then TV President of Warner Bros., continued: "In 2007, The CW was in its infancy and looking for a signature series. These books spoke magnificently well to the possibilities of the network." Dawn Ostroff, then the CW Entertainment Chief, noted that the network was trying to go after a new demographic. "We knew we wanted to go after 18- to 34-year-old women and do scripted content that was going to be bold. *Gossip Girl* fit so many of the characteristics that we were looking for," she said. "It was very easy to see [Schwartz and Savage's] vision. There were so few notes. There's just no way we wouldn't have made this. When we saw their pitch, we thought: 'This is it! This is everything we want!'"

"The way I recall it happening was Alloy [Entertainment] and my agents sent me the *Gossip Girl* books which were set up at The CW already with Dawn Ostroff," Schwartz said on Jessica

Szohr's *XOXO With Jessica Szohr* podcast in 2023. "I immediately called Stephanie [Savage] and said, 'If you like this, let's do this together,' because we were trying to figure out what we were going to do together after *The O.C.* ended and there was nobody I wanted to work with more after that than Steph."

Of already having *Gossip Girl* in mind for the network, Ostroff told *Vanity Fair*,

> We knew we needed the defining show. You have to sort of catch the wind at your back. You have to really hit something that's in the zeitgeist, or really going to matter to people in a way that becomes an emotional connection. And it was even more difficult for us, because we were going after a younger, more finicky audience.

Luckily for Schwartz, Savage, and Ostroff, *Gossip Girl*, the books, were really a thing back in the early 2000s because, to this and many young readers, they were fun and racy and escapist, which is the perfect combination for the young adult fiction that you read under the covers with a flashlight after your parents have gone to sleep and you're not supposed to be awake. It was also bigger than Schwartz and Savage knew, too. Conversations with Ostroff giving *Gossip Girl* the green light ended as *The O.C.* was winding down, and Schwartz recounted being surprised at fan reaction to their next show. "I remember very distinctly being on the set of *The O.C.* finale, and there was a crowd of teenagers in the street," Schwartz told Szohr. "Somebody was like, 'What are you guys going to do next?'"

When he mentioned that *Gossip Girl* would be the next project, Schwartz said, "All these kids screamed! I think we were not fully aware of how big the fan base was, how passionate the fan base was." Little did they know that the little show they were putting together would be the cornerstone of The CW. The network really needed a resurgence following the UPN/WB merger, with fan-favorite shows like *Felicity*, *Dawson's Creek*, and *Gilmore Girls* going off the air. It needed something that felt fresher and sexier than those shows, that offered more aspiration and escapism than the everyday life of a college girl who chased a guy from her high school to NYU (*Felicity*) or the goings-on of teens in a small town in Massachusetts (*Dawson's Creek*).

But putting together *Gossip Girl* didn't come so easily at first. Schwartz said:

> They wanted us to shoot at Warner Brothers [in Los Angeles]. They took us on a tour of the Warner Brothers lot . . . and they took us to Stars Hollow, you know, where they shot *Gilmore Girls*, and they were like, great, this will be Central Park, and there were some New York streets, and we were like. . . . "We can't make the show if it's not set in New York". . . . And then Steph [Savage], being the brilliant producer, figured out how to do it.

Savage explained,

It wasn't that hard. There was like a big tax incentive in New York at the time [to film], and I think everyone at Warner was just nervous about doing a show in New York because they hadn't done it, so it just seemed very like, "Well, how are we going to do that? Like who's going to produce it . . ." And you're like, "People who live in New York . . .?" We got a lot of crew from *The Sopranos* and *Sex and the City*, both of which had recently wrapped shooting.

Schwartz and Savage had made their name in teen television with *The O.C.* and didn't want to be pigeonholed necessarily with this new show, but something about *Gossip Girl* felt fundamentally different than the beachy, "California, here we come" vibes of Ryan Atwood and Seth Cohen and their Newport friends. "Coming off *The O.C.* and getting the *Gossip Girl* books, it was like another teen drama. I feel like we just did this, but it's set in New York and that is cool, and that's a whole other vibe in a different world. And that was for us, the selling point," Schwartz said. After all, who doesn't want to hear about the scandalous lives of rich prep school brats?

Portraying that high school experience meant casting just the right faces to embody the characters of Serena, Blair, Nate, Chuck, Dan, Jenny, and more, and Savage and Schwartz turned to casting director David Rapaport.

"I went in for a meeting on *Gossip Girl*, and I met with Josh and Stephanie . . . I went in with a book of pictures, and I did come up with ideas. I said, 'This is who I sort of picture for Blair and for Nate and for Chuck.'" Rapaport said on *XOXO with Jessica Szohr*, "I don't know that there was anyone that was in that book that ended up being cast, with the exception of Blake [Lively] as Serena. She really was the only one I thought of.... She was perfect for it."

I can't picture another Serena other than Blake Lively, and luckily, Schwartz agreed with Rapaport and me (we're so smart). "We didn't see a lot of other girls for Serena," Schwartz told *Vanity Fair*. "She has to be somebody that you believe would be sitting in the front row at Fashion Week eventually." Lively, who had just appeared in *The Sisterhood of the Traveling Pants*, among other projects, wasn't 100 percent committed to the pace of network television. "I said, 'No, I want to go to college. Thank you, though,'" she told *Vanity Fair*. "Then they said, 'O.K., you can go to Columbia one day a week. After the first year, it'll quiet down. Your life will go back to normal and you can start going to school. We can't put it in writing, but we promise you can go.' So that's why I said, 'O.K. You know what? I'll do this.'" I think we can all say by now we know that her life did not slow down, and she did not go to Columbia, but I think Blake Lively managed to land on her feet, with or without an Ivy League college degree. And she also got to live in New York, too!

"I'm actually a very shy person and the idea of losing my anonymity was one that was scary to me," Lively continued.

"I remember saying when I read this script, 'Whoever does this will not be able to walk out of their house ever again and be the same as before they started this.' You could tell it was a cultural phenomenon. That was both exciting and thrilling, but also very scary."

There was just one thing that didn't land perfectly with the studio when Lively was cast—her sunny, long, flowing, California hair. "Blake's hair was kind of wavy, and some people said, you know, we don't see Blake Lively as an Upper East Side Manhattan girl because she has a sort of wavy hair," Rapaport said.

> And so we had to do a whole screen test with her with very straight hair . . . Josh Schwartz, you know, was the one who really stood up and said, "I have no issue seeing Blake as a New York girl" . . . sometimes it takes doing those screen tests to prove what you see or feel in your heart to executives.

Question—how many actresses' lives have been changed by busting out a flat iron? The world may never know.

Though Serena was in Rapaport's "book," child star and Cindy Lou Who herself Taylor Momsen, who played Jenny, was among the first characters cast, according to Rapaport. It's interesting, though, because Momsen admitted on Penn Badgley's podcast, *Podcrushed*, that she was super hesitant to jump into the whirlwind that would be the show. "I was convinced [to join on], let's put it that way. Larger powers than me came down and went, 'This is a great opportunity,'" she said. "Honestly, the big selling point to me for . . . convincing me to move and wanting to leave school and everything was . . . it's New York . . . you get to move to New York . . . to me, it was just another job . . . I don't think I realized how much of a commitment [a television show] was."

Next came Chuck. "[Ed Westwick] was the only one we considered [for Chuck]. He initially read for Nate, but there was something a little bit more dark and mischievous about him, I think, just off the page. . . . And we brought him in for Chuck and it was like, oh, that's a no brainer," Rapaport said.

"I auditioned in Los Angeles, and then I went home to the UK, and I was sitting with my friends . . . having a drink somewhere and I got the call that I got the job," Westwick told FR Conventions.

> I had to go to New York, and I didn't have a visa! Then I had to go to Canada to get [that] visa . . . and it was crazy and my whole life was about to change. I kind of had a feeling, but I didn't know what this show was going to become . . . I was 19 years old and very excited.

Rapaport remembers Westwick's visa debacle as being slightly more stressful than Westwick lets on. "Ed coming from London, didn't have a visa to work in the States, and his visa did not come through until I think either the day before or the day of his first day of filming on set," he told Szohr.

> Josh and Stephanie, to their credit, would not even look at other tapes that I was sending them, and I would say to them, you guys, like my job was on the line, we have to recast this role because . . . we are not legally allowed to use him. . . . Luckily . . . Ed's visa came through and he was available.

Chuck and his scarves were on their way, but what about Blair, Constance Billard's resident queen bee? "I read with [Leighton] for Blair. . . . She was great, and she walks into the room, and she just has such a presence and is such a star," Rapaport said. "And that was such an exciting find for us . . . I was really excited to discover her in a way. She had worked before, but discover her for this role."

But don't worry—there was even more hair drama surrounding her casting. "Leighton was a blonde when she came in to read, but Blake was the blonde, so we asked her to color her hair," Schwartz told *The Hollywood Reporter*. "A risky move on her part in the middle of pilot season, but she did a sink-rinse dye job to audition as a brunette." You guys, what is it with the hair? Should actresses just carry around a bag of wigs to every audition?

"I started auditioning back in December 2006. The process was really long. At the time, I wanted to move to New York, but I didn't have a reason or any money. So when my agent sent me the *Gossip Girl* script, I thought Blair was perfect for me," Meester told *The Hollywood Reporter*. Chace Crawford, who landed the role of Nate, remembered meeting Leighton and not being able to picture her as Blair because of her blonde vibes. But as soon as she snapped into character, Crawford said, "I just remember thinking, 'That girl can act. She's the perfect girl for this.'" See? Blonde or brunette, be damned.

"Sometimes, no matter how much energy you put in to get a part, you're not going to get it," Meester told *Rolling Stone*. "But this was mine. It felt like mine. So much of me was ready to get this part and move to New York. I'd passed through any bullshit that had happened in my life." Meester wanted Blair badly, and she nailed the audition.

"Chace Crawford was very new and probably read thirty times [for the role of Nate]," Schwartz told *The Hollywood Reporter*. "I went back and forth to countless auditions because [CBS president and CEO] Les Moonves needed to sign off on me," Crawford confirmed to the magazine. He was coming off a failed audition for *Friday Night Lights* and frankly, thought that *Gossip Girl* was a little beneath him. "I kinda went in there with a very kind of blasé [attitude]," Crawford told Alex Cooper on the podcast *Call Her Daddy*. But this rich-kid attitude "probably helped and worked in my favor, as those things kind of do."

Jessica Szohr's casting as Vanessa is the stuff of Hollywood dreams—she was exactly in the right place at the right time. "My friend Nathaniel and Adam were going to a barbecue . . . I was kind of in a weird funk of wanting to move home. I was just kind of over LA," she said on her podcast.

> So [my friends] picked me up, we go to this barbecue, and we were just eating and talking and hanging. And then a couple of days later, my manager called and said, "What did you do this weekend?" And I said, "I was at a barbecue. I went to a movie," and I said, "Um, why what's up?" And she said, "Well, this pilot that is going to launch or you know, get ready to air on The CW, there's a couple episodes, like three or four episodes that they want to see you for."

The host of the barbecue she attended? Josh Schwartz. "I thought it was kind of wild that the entire time we were at that barbecue nothing came up about it . . . that barbecue really changed my life." I have always said that a good hot dog or cheeseburger is life changing, but nothing like this story.

And with that, more featured players on *Gossip Girl* began to find their places on the show. "My commercial agent came to me and was just, like, you should audition for this," Nicole Fiscella, who played Isabel Coates in seasons 1, 2, and 4 told me.

> "They're looking for models for these specific parts, and you know, what do you have to lose?" I had done some commercials and stuff

in the past, so I was like, "OK, fine, what do I have to lose?" It was kind of an interesting thing that happened in the audition, but basically in my very, maybe my last audition . . . it was auditioning with a girl . . . and I don't know why they kind of paired us together. I remember that Josh and Stephanie were there, but I didn't know who they were at that point. At that point, I'm sure everybody else who went in was just like, oh, these are like major producers. And I had no idea. So I started to read the lines, and the other girl started reading lines and I was, like, "What is she saying?" I'm like, "This is not the scene we're reading at all." So, I stopped and I looked at her. I looked at her pages, her sides, and I was just, like, "oh, my gosh, I'm just like, you have all these boy parts here. These are not the parts you are supposed to have!" And everybody's just sort of dying. And I didn't even realize what I was saying. It's just like, that's my personality. I just kind of, you know, off the cuff, saying stuff and everyone started laughing. And I think that's what really clinched it for me.

Sam Robards, who played Nate's dad, Howard "The Captain" Archibald, took the job of Nate's drug-addled, embezzling dad mostly because he needed the cash and had some time (which IMO is very, very Howard-coded of him). "Listen, I had a *day* on the pilot episode. Two lines! I was like, 'All right, I'm in New York, I just got back, I'll do it. I don't know what the hell's going on,'" he told Broadway.com. "All of a sudden they want me for another one, and another and another. Suddenly [my character] is doing blow, swilling whiskey, punching his kid! I'm walking down the street and girls are going, 'Omigod, are you Nate's dad?!'" Robards' nonchalance probably helped his portrayal, because 90 percent of the words Captain Archibald said on *Gossip Girl* were a lie, so it didn't even matter what Robards said—just that he could act.

I know we all want to know how fan-favorite maid, caretaker, and Blair confidante Dorota got her spot on the show. "When I auditioned, Dorota had no lines in that first episode.... So when I went in, I had to improvise because there was no text to audition with, so I kind of like played my Polish part because I was born in Poland, and I was raised by Polish parents who spoke Polish at home," recalled Zuzanna Szadkowski, who played Dorota. "So I went ahead and did a lot of, like, muttering under my breath in Polish. And maybe that's what got me the part . . . I kind of knew it would be buzzy, but I had no idea if I would have anything substantial to do. I was happy to have a job, but I didn't know what to expect."

With most of the teenagers and younger folk on the show locked into place, Schwartz and Savage knew that they needed grownups to anchor the show, and though they had to fight for more money for Matthew Settle [Rufus] and Kelly Rutherford [Lily] to join, it was worth it. "It was important," Schwartz told *The Hollywood Reporter*. Schwartz and Savage had just come off *The O.C.*, which seemed to feature as many grownups as kids, but *Gossip Girl*'s prep school setting doesn't really lend itself to adding a lot of adults unless it was going to be in a *Never Been Kissed*, undercover student, "how do you do, fellow kids?" sort of way. By nailing down the important adults (and one of the show's main shippable couples), *Gossip Girl* wasn't just going to be some sort of MTV *Spring Break* party on the Upper East Side. Also, the grownups are usually the ones that dole out the punishments, which, if these snotty kids act out, they need some consequences, right?

Lily Van Der Woodsen, aka Kelly Rutherford, is as graceful and unflappable IRL as she is on television and on Instagram, where she is now a style celebrity. "Kelly, I remember, came into the audition, and she had her baby, like she came in with the stroller, and I think like one of my assistants held the baby in the other room while she was auditioning," Rapaport said to Szohr. "And that's like, it's hard to audition. I can't imagine how actors do it like that. You just, you have to drive all over town and be available and memorize, you know, fifteen pages of sides. When you have a young child, it's a wild kind of crazy."

Bucky Barnes—sorry, Sebastian Stan, who played Carter Baizen—admitted he was pretty nervous about the show. "I was scared!" he said on Penn Badgley's *Podcrushed* podcast. "First of all, I knew Chace [Crawford], but otherwise I didn't know anybody. . . . *Gossip Girl* was everything. I felt like it was the new *Sex and the City*."

Gossip Girl didn't have as many adult actors as Schwartz and Savage's previous show, *The O.C.*, but they added a bit of glam to the largely teenage cast.

The CW Network/Photofest © The CW Network.

Michelle Trachtenberg, who passed away in February 2025, played Georgina Sparks. She only needed to hear two words on the phone to agree to the part: "Evil bitch." "The phone call sort of went like, hey, do you want to come on this show that people hadn't fully heard of, but still because it also stopped airing [because of the writers strike]?" she told Szohr. "I had just finished this film and I'm like, 'Okay, well what's the character about?' 'Well, we can tell you she's an evil bitch.' And I'm like, oh, and okay, you had me at evil."

With most of the cast locked in, the last spot was Lonely Boy himself, Dan Humphrey, and the person that Rapaport had in mind was not Penn Badgley. "I was obsessed with this kid,

Alden Ehrenreich, who a lot of you probably know from the *Star Wars* movies now . . . I remember I really desperately wanted to come in for this role, and he actually passed on it, because his parents said 'we want him to go to college, and we don't want him to do TV,'" Rapaport said to Szohr. "He did a phenomenal, phenomenal audition. I thought he was such a star. And the producers . . . just said he's too short for Blake, like he could maybe play the brother, but I don't see him being the love [interest]. . . . And Penn was the last one to be cast."

"I had worked with Penn Badgley [on a WB pilot] and had told him several times to stop doing WB pilots," Savage told Szohr. "Then I had to go back and say, 'OK, one more!'" According to *Rolling Stone*, Badgley needed convincing just like Blake Lively did, noting he was "cynical" about television. He made the decision over a weekend to do the show. "Stephanie and Josh know how to walk the line between creative integrity and commercial sensibility," he said at the time.

After that marathon of casting, questions remained—would the cast have chemistry beyond the pilot? Would this recently assembled cast of unknowns and established actors have what it took to break through in a crowded television season? The answer was, instantly, yes.

"Not to pat ourselves on the back, but I think we did do a good job of kind of matching the essence of the character to the person in some ways. And they were, not to say that these people were their characters, they're obviously all playing roles and what have you, but the essence of them was there," Rapaport said. "I think . . . [chemistry] is one of those things that you hope for in every show that you cast. . . . We got lucky. We got very lucky." Of those beginning days on set, Savage said she knew they had magic. "We all went to see [the movie] *Blades of Glory* and [we were] walking with them [and thinking], 'I don't know what the rest of the world is going to think, [but] when I see these kids together, I feel excited,'" she told *Vanity Fair*.

As Rapaport was doing the casting, Schwartz and Savage, who had fought so hard to ensure that *Gossip Girl* was being filmed in New York, were fighting to score the best possible locations for the show.

"When we were making the pilot . . . nobody knew what the show was. We could shoot in like Grand Central Station, you know, like that was an actual New York location, but everybody else was like 'no' [to letting us film]," Schwartz told Szohr. "[The manager at the Palace Hotel] was like, 'I read the script and I think it's fabulous.' He was so in on the show. So that's why we're at the Palace. And from the Palace, everything kind of built from there, too. Then people were, you know, knocking down the door being like, can we shoot here?"

The people and the places were there. The stories were being written. The fans of the book series were excited. But would the viewers come?

ORIGINS

This image was everywhere to promote *Gossip Girl*'s first season. Each season brought forth a new marketing campaign, some reviled by parents and critics as too risqué.

Photo by Timothy White/The CW Network/Photofest © The CW Network.

Why the Pilot of *Gossip Girl* is One of the Best Pilots of All Time

I love TV. I have always watched a lot of television, so much so, that if you tell me you don't own a television, I can't even agree to disagree. (And don't do the "BuT i WaTcH tV oN mY cOmPuTeR iNsTeAd," because that is still watching a big glowing screen that shouts at you. It's a technicality and it counts. You have a TV.) If you're missing out on watching TV, you're missing out on comedy, drama, beauty, joy, pain, laughter, and the broadening of new worlds. I watch so much TV that I find myself especially equipped to judge show after show, and that's why I'm qualified to announce, here and now, that *Gossip Girl*'s pilot episode is among the best TV pilots of all time.

You've probably had it happen—you and a friend or someone you get stuck talking to at a party are making idle chit chat when the topic of shows comes up. They recommend some series, but they say, "The first season is a little rough . . . it takes a while to get into it." Um, get out of here, please. With so many viewing options these days, I'm not waiting eight episodes to get "into" a show. It's like a soufflé—it's either ready or it's not. And *Gossip Girl*, come hell or high water, was ready to go from the first frame.

Thanks to Mark Piznarski's directing, the opening five minutes set the stage tonally and in a cinematographic sense for the entire series, which is more than most shows can say. It really knew what it was from the very beginning.

"I had a specific thing I wanted to do . . . I had just seen [Sofia Coppola's] *Marie Antoinette* . . . and I really liked how they took the old-time settings, castles, and gowns and stuff, but the kids all acted like they do in 2007," he recalled. "[On *Gossip Girl* I thought], we have the modern kids already, but we'll drape them in jewels and palaces, so that they can be themselves, but in a castle. That was kind of always, in my mind, stylistically to try to put them in environments [like that] as much as possible."

Gossip Girl's pilot immediately throws you right into the action—we open with big, sweeping shots of New York City, unmistakable in its size and grandeur, and slowly focus on Serena Van Der Woodsen's beautiful face and jauntily tied neck scarf zipping toward Manhattan on the Metro-North train from her boarding school in Connecticut. Would such a rich kid be taking public transit? Does it matter? No. The whistling tune of Peter Bjorn and John's "Young Folks" plays. And then the one, the only, our omniscient narrator Gossip Girl pops in, pseudo-stalking Serena at Grand Central Station and calling out that she's gonna be watching the rest of you, too. "I think we were the first ones to actually use cell phones as part of a TV show," Piznarski told me. "It's ubiquitous now. . . . We didn't want to do it in a boring way, filming a screen and sitting there, having people read it as long as it takes to read. There was always a narrator in the books, right? So, we knew that we could use that and we knew it had to be Kristen Bell."

Given the celebrity tabloid culture that permeated, stinkily, the culture of the 2000s, this "we're always watching" vibe wasn't exactly new. Perez Hilton and Gawker Stalked abounded. But *Gossip Girl* changed the "we"—it wasn't the bloggers and the magazine people and the paparazzi but basically anyone on the street that could capture you doing something they deemed interesting. It put the power back into the hands of the people. That idea has evolved into an entirely different animal now—you have to remember that *Gossip Girl* was pre-iPhone. Today, everyone doesn't just have a camera in their pockets—they have a camera that can film a crisp, clear, feature-length film. I can't say that *Gossip Girl*'s creators knew what the world would become nearly twenty years later, but if they have a crystal ball, do they have lottery numbers they can share?

Of course, the pilot has issues typical for any pilot, mostly of the continuity variety: Blair's mother was recast between the pilot and the rest of the series. Blair's apartment is totally different. Nate had Patrick Bateman hair and Chuck had a brutal Caesar chop. Actually, come to think of it, Dan's hair was too short, too. (Thankfully, the mane issues were worked out quickly.) Chuck mentions his mother in the pilot (but he doesn't have one, even though that's complicated). In "the more things change, the more they stay the same" news, Chuck sleeps with his father's employees, who are definitely not in a position to say no to him and keep their jobs, and he's sexually aggressive towards Serena and tries to assault Jenny. The show treats Brooklyn like it's a developing nation (by 2007, it was already a hot zone with gentrifying neighborhoods), and somehow, Chuck and Nate, heirs to literal dynasties, take an MTA bus to school. And don't get me started on 16-year-olds preferring martinis—I'm more than double Serena's age and can't stomach them.

And yet, and yet, *Gossip Girl* and its pilot were a harbinger of what was to come. A nation of voyeurs and chatter and misinformation, all fed to us by "I am Oz the great and powerful"-level voices. It was glitz, it was glam, it was everything viewers needed.

2

WRITING, RECEPTION, AND RECAPS

Gossip Girl had its locations, its cast, and the full support of The CW behind it, but would anyone even watch it? "Good" viewing numbers in 2007 were different from what they are now, because today's viewers have so many more options in not just what they watch but *where* they watch. In 2007, there were no streaming services and less widespread adoption of things like DVR. It's true that Nielsen—the crème de la crème of measuring viewership—started tracking "time-shifted viewing," i.e., people watching their shows not live but later, in 2005. Unfortunately, advertisers pushed back—mostly because it would cost them more money to showcase their wares (more eyes watching one airing of a show = higher advertising rates)—and a lot of networks were ignoring those numbers. Plus, viewers had to wait as long as a week until episodes of their favorite shows were available online to download and watch. It was only in 2017 that Nielsen started including certain streamers in their ratings—so even though the beginnings of a huge cultural shift in how we all consumed media were present in 2007, no one cared to truly measure it until a decade later.

What we know now is that time-shifted viewing hugely impacts ratings, but back then, this sort of traditional thinking negatively affected youth-oriented programs, smaller budget shows, and smaller networks. For something to stay on the air, it needed to be a bona fide hit or it would just get canceled. *Gossip Girl* premiered on September 19, 2007, and 3.5 million people watched it. To compare, 7.1 million people watched a special episode of *Grey's Anatomy* on that same night, and 8.4 million people watched a rerun of *Criminal Minds*. "It was incredibly frustrating. Nielsen doesn't have a great grasp on measuring younger viewers. You couldn't go anywhere in the country without finding people obsessed with the show," Dawn Ostroff, then president of The CW, told *Vanity Fair*. "Where *Gossip Girl* ranked No. 100 on the Nielsen list, it was No. 13 when you looked at the power-content ratings: a combination of Nielsen ratings, traffic online, and buzz."

Ostroff was correct—*Gossip Girl*'s original ratings were middling, but it was rated in the Top 10 New Shows on Awareness by OTX Research during the 2007–8 television season. People knew it existed, and there was online buzz about it. Critical reviews dubbed the show more of a guilty pleasure than an hour of must-see prestige television, but it was smart enough and funny enough for them. The reviews weren't all-out pans, and

WRITING, RECEPTION, AND RECAPS

what young people read reviews and take them seriously anyway? In the end, an event that killed dozens of other shows was the accelerant that helped *Gossip Girl* catch fire—the 2007–8 Writers Guild of America strike.

Lasting from November 5, 2007, to February 12, 2008—a whopping one hundred days—the writers' strike broke down production in every entertainment facet of the country. No one was writing, no one was casting, no one was filming. There was no new episodic output, so The CW and all the other networks were forced to do the one thing they didn't really want to do: run reruns all day, every day.

"The CW, because they couldn't just run repeats or game shows, [*Gossip Girl* was] all they had," co-creator Josh Schwartz told *Vanity Fair*. "They kept re-running the show during the strike so more and more people were watching." There are only so many Nick at Nite episodes a person can take in, so why not tune into the newest, sexiest show of the season and catch up for when it all comes back?

"We had not completed our first run before the strike started . . . I think we had maybe 10 or 12 episodes that aired before we couldn't write anymore . . . and then because they didn't have anything else to show they repeated those episodes over and over again . . . and that really helped our popularity," Savage said on *The Selfish Gift* podcast. "They did like a behind-the-scenes of *Gossip Girl* special they aired before the new episodes aired [after the strike] and that felt impactful."

This is when the famous "OMFG" marketing campaign came into play, with images of the scantily clad cast with "OMFG" layered on top of them halfway through Season 1, in the spring of 2008. This would be followed by a campaign featuring phrases from critical reviews and parental complaints, like "Every parent's nightmare" and "Mind-blowingly inappropriate," ahead of Season 2.

"We hadn't liked the marketing campaign that they'd done for Season 1 at all," Savage said.

> It was just like, very generic and confusing . . . when they brought [the show] back after the strikes, we got a second marketing campaign that used images from the show and it used pull quotes saying, "every parent's worst nightmare" and all of the bad things that people said about the show. They used them as quotes in the promotion with these really beautiful, lush images . . . the contrast pushed the show into the next level.

The CW wanted to reintroduce viewers to the show, and boy, did they make it eye-catching. Rick Haskins, then The CW's executive vice president of marketing and digital programs, told *Vulture*, "This idea was inspired by taking a deep research dive into viewer's social-media usage and understanding how and what they were talking about the show. The sexier tone was based on what was resonating with the audience and mirroring it back." Parenting groups and critics around the country hated it and protested the show, but we all know what happens when you promote censorship—it just drives more eyes to what you're trying to erase in the first place. Haskins admitted it "added fuel" to the fire of *Gossip Girl*'s increasing viewership. When the show came back following the resolution of the writers' strike, "people knew what the show was," executive producer Joshua Safran told *Vanity Fair*. "By playing back the negative quotes about the show using visuals from the show, we hit the perfect tone," Haskins said. "The audience loved the juxtaposition of headline and visual, and it reinforced to them why they watched the show their parents hated."

And then it was off to the races to ensure people kept coming back for more, which meant ensuring the writing was on par. "[The books] were heightened in a way that Josh [Schwartz] and I didn't feel would translate to TV. As you get deeper in the books, like, Chuck Bass has a monkey . . . Dan Humphrey was, like, a punk rock singer," Savage said on *The Selfish Gift* podcast. "We really used the first book as a jumping off point for establishing the characters [and] we made some important shifts [in storytelling] to try to make the characters feel more grounded and likeable which I think helped sort of draw people in."

Lasher told me,

> We wrote the show in Los Angeles and shot the show in New York, and we would go to New York for our episodes. In the beginning, we would only go for like a few days, but as the time

went on, we would be more involved in the producing. In the writers' room, yes, like we were very there. There was this feeling that we had captured something, especially the first season, they captured something with these OMFG moments, and the show needed to maintain that.

So we would talk about stories within that context a lot like, you know, we wanted to make sure that the show really delivered on these moments that felt transgressive and exciting and fun, but also within the realm of what the show is. [We didn't want to] feel like we were jumping the shark . . . we wanted to make sure that it felt real within the characters that we had established and within the world of the show. [But it was a] heightened thing and that definitely did drive storytelling.

Rewatching the episodes now as an adult who remembers the good old days of New York City in the mid-to-late 2000s, I am still quite amazed at the attention to detail that the writers kept up for so long. I was not in the mindset at the time to go clubbing in Manhattan during the show's original airing, but upon rewatch, the writers constantly made references to very New York restaurants, clubs, people, places, and things. Even though a lot of the writers were in Los Angeles, they really understood New York City in a way that you would think is hard to do from three thousand miles away.

And the references were a lot of the fun. "*Gossip Girl* in my memory was like the first show to do that [Easter egging]. To put in so many references, so many insider references that were designed to be clickbait. . . . Obviously, their goal was this cultural permeation that they talk about all the time," said journalist Jessica Pressler.

> They did such a great job of seizing on all of these things, like they kind of picked up where *Sex and the City* left off with like, really good clothes on TV. They just did a really good job of insinuating themselves into the culture and becoming this viral show in a way . . . it was a fun show, you know, it was a drama, but it was also, it was really a comedy on a lot of levels.

These Easter eggs and meme-able moments were prescient for the moments shows and brands try to create to go "viral" on TikTok, Instagram, and more. Can you imagine if this show had been around for TikTok? The audios that would have been made available for lip-syncing and dancing. I'm just picturing an army of cats or zoo animals doing the acapella version of "Glamorous" by Fergie.

"Fun" is the refrain of many of the fans, cast, and crew when they speak about *Gossip Girl*. For all of the soapy drama, there were a lot of tongue-in-cheek moments, a lot of winking to the audience and to themselves, whether it be a New York City inside joke or a subtle reference to something from a season before. *Gossip Girl* was on television at the same time as serious shows like *Mad Men* and *Breaking Bad*, so it was the perfect choice for viewers who wanted something that was still smart but not quite so self-referential and serious. *Gossip Girl* never played down like some sort of goofy network sitcom, but it understood that, at its core, it was a teen soap opera with pretty people and pretty outfits. It was escapism that wasn't totally stupid.

Producer Josh Safran told *BuddyTV* that writing for each member of the cast stretched the writers' room's collective brain in different ways:

> Each couple, be it Dan and Serena, Lily and Rufus, Chuck and Blair, each one represents different things we love writing, seeing play out. Chuck and Blair are our longest standing teen couple on the show, so their dynamic is going to reflect that, their history, their issues, but I feel like when you look back, Serena and Dan also had amazing chemistry. . . . Just like Nate and Dan have great friend chemistry together. Their scenes together always make me smile. Writing for Chuck and Blair takes a different part of your brain, the more dastardly, manipulative, bon-mot tossing part, but I'm also grateful to be able to write Serena's knowing sense of humor, her soul searching, her strength, Jenny's bold determination and irreverence, Rufus' steadfastness. All the different sides to each character and coupling is what makes the show interesting, and I don't weigh one over another.

"Finding each character's vulnerable moments like that always felt like a really exciting hat trick to be like, 'Oh, we've had this character do these terrible things. How do we then find the humanity and make the audience care and not sell out the character?' I always really enjoyed that play because it is a balance," Lasher said.

It was through this balance that the universal themes of *Gossip Girl* played out. These were super-rich kids, with trust funds and private schools and all the privilege that the world could give them, and Chuck was still hoping his dad would love him. Dan was still pining away for a girl who didn't know who he was. Jenny was struggling to find herself. Blair was worried about her boyfriend. Just regular-people stuff, even though the outside was more polished and pretty.

Though sassy and funny, there was also a softness to the interpersonal relationships that was really appealing, too. According to Zuzanna Szadkowski, who played Dorota:

[My character's] first appearance is Blair sort of like spilling her heart to someone. And you assume it's to her mother because of the tone of the conversation. And then, you know, then the shot is wide and zooms out, and you see that it's the housekeeper. And I feel like at that moment, you know, you have this relationship, so it's like paid staff, but they're having to take on a sort of a maternal role and a caretaker role. And like, you know, it sort of had, I feel like there was so much information and just the way that they set up their relationships. It started there and then grew . . . Dorota was a little bit of a moral center or a sort of a soft place for Blair to fall.

Another difficult writing moment came when Taylor Momsen, who played Jenny, expressed interest in leaving *Gossip Girl* in

Season 4. "[Acting] was a childhood thing that I got put into at 2 years old. I wasn't making my own choices then," she told Penn Badgley on *Podcrushed*. "Literally, as soon as I got to an age where I could make my own decisions, it was like a click . . . I woke up one morning and went, 'Wait a second. I don't have to do this? I don't have to do this other job? I can just play in my band and tour and write songs? I can just do that?'"

But just leaving a hit network show as a series regular is a little more difficult than just quitting—with storyboards and plans already drawn up for each season and contracts drafted and signed, Momsen couldn't just walk away and write music.

"It was hard at a certain point to write for the old Jenny; we had to write for the new Taylor," Safran told *Vulture*. "Taylor wanted her hair a certain way because she was in the band and that was who she was, so we couldn't dye Taylor's hair to be Jenny every day, especially when she had events where she had to be Taylor for the weekend. So Jenny had to change."

As Momsen pushed to do her music career full-time and leave acting behind, Schwartz and Savage acquiesced and she was written off. "At a certain point, she just felt like she didn't want to be an actress anymore, which, considering how young she was when she started on the show, was something that we felt like we had to be respectful of," said Savage.

Today, Momsen is grateful that Savage and Schwartz changed their *Gossip Girl* stories so that she could write her own. "[It was] a little more complicated to get out of a television show,"

WRITING, RECEPTION, AND RECAPS

Momsen said on *Podcrushed*. "[Production] went, 'Well, we can't let you out of your deal, but we can write you out of the show so you can go on tour. You can't act in anything else, though.' They really allowed me to follow my dream, and I'm forever grateful and thankful to them for that."

While the writers' room was researching and penning the iconic stories that would appear on our televisions, co-creator Stephanie Savage was working behind the scenes to make sure the luxe world of Manhattan's elite always looked like old money, even if the production budget was more beer-and-chips than champagne and caviar.

"For Lily's wedding, which was the end of Season One, I'm cooking up like what this wedding should be, which is like, literally a million dollar wedding," Savage told Szohr.

> It's gonna be outside in the garden at the Frick [Museum in New York], and she needs a Vera Wang dress . . . we've got to do [this and] that, and then uh, our line producer's . . . going like, we cannot afford this. . . . So it was like, well, will Vera Wang give us a dress if you know, we say Vera Wang? And that was kind of the beginning of doing that, and then it really grew to you know, everybody in town wanting a cameo. . . . And I don't know that anybody ever said no to us.

"Stephanie . . . figured out how to get so much money on the screen and product integrations . . . we shot in the Hamptons in the Season Two premiere, which is very expensive and hard to do," Schwartz added.

> There may have been a pyramid of Vitamin Water in the background, but it paid for it, and Stephanie figured that out. And Stephanie's dream was to shoot an episode in Paris. And everybody's like, you're insane. There's literally no way you'll ever be able to afford shooting in Paris [in Season 4], and Stephanie's like, well, I'm going to show you.

And show them Savage did, even getting exclusive filming access for Paris's most famous landmarks. "*Gossip Girl* got us into places. We were the first show to ever film in the Musée D'Orsay," director Mark Piznarski said.

> They had never let anyone film in there. Then they heard the words "*Gossip Girl*" and [we're] in the door. And it was on a Monday, and it was closed, and while we're setting up for something, I'm walking around and I'm seeing that, you know, the famous Van Gogh [self-portrait], and I can reach out and touch it, and I'm just thinking, I can't believe that I get to do this just cause because I'm, you know, the director of *Gossip Girl*. It's just amazing. . . . And it's like the curtains parted, the ropes came down, and in you went.

At the same time, the online mania about *Gossip Girl* was growing higher and higher, thanks largely in part to weekly episodic recaps on *New York Magazine*'s Daily Intel blog, written

WRITING, RECEPTION, AND RECAPS

by journalists Jessica Pressler and Chris Rovzar and expounded upon by a frenetic commentariat. For an OG *Gossip Girl* fan such as myself, the recaps were as big a draw as the episodes themselves. The format was pretty simple—Rovzar and Pressler would talk about the high points of the episode, then do a "Reality Index," giving points values to plot details that were not plausible, dead-on, mediocre, unbelievable, and more. For example, being able to get from Serena's Upper East Side dwelling to Dan's Brooklyn loft in twenty minutes would earn a negative score, because that's not happening unless you're going by helicopter (and we all know the Humphreys couldn't afford a helicopter). But teenagers overtaking Bungalow 8, a club that was then past its prime, earned a positive score because it was so realistic. The show and the recaps had a growing symbiotic relationship, and soon, a mass of witty commenters would leave their own thoughts and ratings at the bottom of the recap. Back then, the move was to read the initial recap, then wait and go back for the best of the comments to be filled in. Then, there would be another post about all of the best comments—it just went on and on in a wave of viral fun.

Like most online viral moments, Pressler and Rovzar never knew their recaps would become so big. "When [producers] conceived of *Gossip Girl*, this city was in a major economic boom. It was like super flashy wealth . . . the Meatpacking District was no longer slaughterhouses, but bottle service clubs," Pressler said. "You had these glass buildings popping up left and right.

Just really flashy, like huge amounts of money in Manhattan, so it definitely came out of that era and it fit in with that era like it made sense like, oh, they're doing this now."

"Chris and I had just started at Daily Intel, which was a blog. . . . Our job was to blog basically, like the news of New York, but neither of us were real hard news people. We were looking for fun stuff to write about," she continued. "And when [*Gossip Girl*] came out, it was Chris's idea to do this 'Reality Index' because he had heard that they were . . . name dropping clubs like Butter and stuff like that. That was his idea to kind of be like, 'how does it measure up to real life?'"

Rovzar said,

The way we ran Daily Intel at the time, it was very much about New York stuff, so anything that was in the culture, that was about the city, we wanted to follow. And so we watched the first episode [of *Gossip Girl*] just to kind of see what it was like, and there was so much New York in it. We were actually surprised, and we thought, "oh, let's just, like, write about the New York of it, getting around, and can you get from point A to point B and in 5 minutes, would people really go to that restaurant?" And so we just did one recap of the first episode, and people liked it and we kept doing it.

Because *Gossip Girl* was so popular, it wasn't surprising that the recaps caught fire, too. "[There was this] huge comment gang of people who would love to add their own little observations and things . . . because everybody was watching [*Gossip Girl*] and noticing the same thing. . . . It was almost like a gamified show," Pressler said.

"It was like a C plot that was running with all of the New York insider stuff. It was very, very popular right away. It got the most traffic out of anything that we did. And so [*New York Magazine* was] like, well, you have to keep doing it."

Rovzar added,

> It was very cool to know that there was a response to the recaps because the recaps were really powered not only by us, watching the show and pausing it every two seconds, but by all the commenters, the *New York Magazine* commenters who would write in all their own stuff in the comments section, and then we would run at the end of the week a "recap of the recap," and we would do the best comments and we would give them points.

I happened to be one of those commenters—these recaps were a big reason why I became such a *Gossip Girl* fan, namely because a smart, funny show attracted a smart, funny commentariat. I lurked more than I participated, but honestly, it felt like most of the highest scoring commenters on the Daily Intel recaps could have written for *Gossip Girl*. I was always obsessed with pop culture in all forms, but watching people write about pop culture and then comment on pop culture and then write about them commenting on pop culture. . . . It was all very, "This is a career path?" (And now you're reading my book! On *Gossip Girl*! Crazy!)

In 2007, we didn't have the unrelenting chatter of social media that we have in 2026. As you'll read in the next chapter, the only real online community that one could build for a show was in an online fan forum, and for most of that, you really had to dig. Writers and producers of shows could get immediate feedback solely through ratings, so you can imagine that *Gossip Girl*'s writers and producers jumped on reading the *Daily Intel* recaps as soon as they could. Personally, I'm of the mindset that you should never, ever read the comment sections, because today it's where good sense goes to die and troll farms come to roost, but in 2007, it was a different vibe.

"We definitely read the recaps, because you have to understand at the time, like social media wasn't there," Lasher said. "You didn't have the same sort of fan interaction. And so to have something like that was so much fun because even though it was [media], it still felt like you were interacting with the fans."

"I heard the writers talking about it in the room after the pilot aired. Josh Safran sent me a link. I remember reading, thinking it was clever and funny—cooler than a recap! Obsessed with New York, just like us!" Savage told *Vulture* in 2012. "And [they] got it completely. . . . And thus reading the Index and the comments became a Tuesday-morning ritual."

The cast couldn't escape the charms of the internet, either. "I [was] known to get to the NYMag site too early on a Tuesday and to have to refresh, refresh, refresh until the recap [came] up," Szadkowski, told *Vulture*. "Thank goodness for the army of astute commenters who would never let me down. If I was ever in need of Dorota love, I just had to scroll down."

"After each episode, they would write what was like real New York and what was fake, and they would kind of like, do a breakdown of the episode . . . [before this], I wrote episodes of TV, and the feedback just wasn't there," Lasher told Szohr.

> There were ratings or, you know, people would be fans that you'd meet sometimes, but on *Gossip Girl*, interaction with the fans and the media was so heightened and immediate, and it was exciting and it was cool to see people respond and react. It was such a moment that was happening that we were all part of and experiencing in these different ways.

"[The recaps] changed our life . . . put us on the map in a lot of ways," former CW President Dawn Ostroff told *Vulture*. "I can honestly tell you that [the recaps] had a huge influence on that show being a success. And I always thought [they] were very fair. . . . But Stephanie and Josh will have things to say. They're so particular, and they have excellent memories. Good or bad, they'll carry the grudge."

Grudge or not, these recaps, depending on who you ask, led to a pseudo-dialogue among Pressler, Rovzar, and the commenters and the *Gossip Girl* producers and writers, leading some (including me) to speculate that the writers and producers would change stories based on the reactions and direct requests of the recappers and commentariat.

"We got in touch with the writers pretty early because we did that story when the show came back for the second season, so we knew Stephanie and Josh," Rovzar said. "They kind of indicated, as I recall, that they read the recaps and sort of kept track of them. As the years went on, we got more of a sense that they read them every week and it was a fun thing to talk about."

"We like to think that they included stuff for us, but I don't know that they really did," Pressler said. "I know that they talked about it, because I had conversations later with Josh Safran and other people. I know that they talked about like, 'Oh, the Reality Index is going to kill us for this.' I don't think we influenced any storylines."

They at least influenced some of the show's outfits. "My team and I read it aloud every Tuesday morning, almost religiously, usually with giggles and smirks, sometimes with scowls as our fabulous fashions were scrutinized," costume designer Eric Daman told *Vulture*. "The Cleavage Rhombus really had a mind of its own and would show up unexpectedly, but definitely gained more attention once NYMag named it. We totally tried to push the Rhombus Index beyond its original Herve Leger traffic-stopping appearance to the ultimate, 'can't-go-any further-without-an-R-rating,' perfectly framed in a Maxime Simoens cut-out tux jacket." (And FYI, the Cleavage Rhombus was an ongoing joke from Pressler and Rovzar about Serena's wardrobe, which always seemed to feature at least one outfit per episode with a large cut-out over her chest. It was the 2000s, ok? It was cut-outs, bandage dresses, and Ed Hardy faux-tattoo tees as far as the eye can see. Actually, I think most of that is making a comeback. . . .)

Mostly fun and helpful, that is. "As much as we loved when the Index or commenters mentioned something we felt the same way about, it was incredibly vexing when something we'd done was misinterpreted or didn't come across," Savage told *Vulture*.

> There were a zillion times I wanted to explain or clarify, to defend with documentation or at least narrate the process as to why we made a certain choice. . . . Because it wasn't like we didn't talk about this stuff. We had giant fights in the scout van about Dan Humphrey's transit route to St. Jude's. We made the writer's assistant call a marina to find out how people get their mail delivered when they are traveling around the world on a yacht. . . . It is totally realistic that Chuck Bass would take the bus like he does in the pilot (weekday mornings, all the real-life CB's gather in front of the Ralph Lauren store on Madison, waiting to ride to the Nineties). But we also kind of loved that somehow a 16-year-old being chauffeured around in his own stretch limo ended up seeming more realistic, because of who Chuck became as a character.

"I can't remember which episode the pierogies were in . . . but they gave negative points about the veracity of Vanessa going all the way to the East Village to Veselka to get pierogies and then *back* to Brooklyn. They are totally right," writer Jessica Queller told *Vulture*. "The Veselka reference was so true to my experience of being young in NYC in the early nineties. But that was before everyone I knew migrated to Brooklyn. Totally unrealistic that Vanessa would have schlepped to the East Village." (And it is! Why would she take the L train back and forth ten times a day? She could find insanely good pierogies in Greenpoint right in front of her face!)

"I don't remember us sort of changing anything based on them . . . I remember there being times where I would be like, 'oh, yeah, that's fair,' if it was a critique," Lasher said. "But I mean, they were so much fun, and their love of the show was so clear that it, nobody was upset by it, you know, and it was a really fun way to feel like we were interacting with the audience because we were having so much fun."

The biggest complaint from this writer about the show's unrealistic storylines is one Rovzar still shares, too. "No one ever picked up the phone to call anybody. There's a lot of [showing up at] people's doors without calling," he joked.

I see this "did-they-or-didn't-they" use of the recaps to inform the writers' room both ways. Because as a creative, you put yourself out there, on the line, to the world, every time you produce a piece of art. (So be nice to me when you read this book. I'm just a girl.) The writers and producers and cast and crew of *Gossip Girl* are doing the jobs they love, only to get torn down on the internet, nay, on a small blog offshoot of a magazine website, by commenters who are at home, furiously typing, leaving Cool Ranch Dorito dust all over their keyboards. There have been chat rooms since the early days of the internet, but *Gossip Girl*'s already fiery online fervor meant that its fans were commenting more, early, and often. There was a lot more to say online about a show in which the entire plot meant everyone needed to be online.

But if *Gossip Girl* wanted to be the sexy, smart, witty, in-the-know show it always claimed to be, certain details like "it should take much longer to get from the Upper East Side to Brooklyn" (sorry, as a former New York City resident with friends in Brooklyn, this one always ground my gears) could have at least been winked at. Like, "Man, that took way too long on the train!" Or, "My limo got stuck in traffic!" Or something. Can you have your finger on the pulse of an entire city in a television show and leave realism behind? Where does realism end and TV begin? What kinds of things should the commentariat call out, and what should they leave alone?

With *Gossip Girl* began the ouroboros that TV writers and, hell, creators in general have needed to manage since social media became ubiquitous. The snake is now eating its own tail, because artists want people to talk about the art that they're creating, and they want them to be passionate about it . . . but not too passionate and not too mean about it, either. They don't want fans to point out too many plot holes or start obviously racist campaigns against newly cast leads. (I'm looking at you, *Star Wars*.) But a lack of online engagement and buzz can break an otherwise artistically good project. *Gossip Girl* was among the first shows to have to answer to a wildly rabid fan base in real time, and perhaps that's why it jumped the shark at the end. That's how we ended up with Dan as Gossip Girl—because the other Gossip Girls the creators allegedly had in mind were spoiled by fans and tabloids. Was the call coming from inside the house?

No matter where you fall on either side of this debate, it's safe to say that there were some real duds when it came to storytelling on *Gossip Girl*. The Ivy/Lola inheritance plot, with Carol trying to scam her sister and William and Ivy trying to take everyone down but not really? And then Rufus dating Ivy, who could be his daughter? Rufus and Lily's love child, Scott, who they said, "Come back any time!" and he just . . . never did? Juliet Sharp and her revenge on Serena? Armie Hammer and his Ponzi scheme with Poppy Lifton, a name that only makes me think of Lipton tea? Though the show was always balancing a lot of plots at one time, it's OK to say that they couldn't all be winners. (Don't worry, I've rated my best and worst *Gossip Girl* storylines of all time on page 64.)

WRITING, RECEPTION, AND RECAPS

Writer and *Gossip Girl* superfan Tyler McCall said:

The Prince Louis one [where Blair was really in love with Chuck but married Louis anyway]. It's less that I throw it in the trash. . . . It overstayed its welcome. There are a couple storylines that kind of overstayed their welcome . . . one was the [Juliet Sharp] one. One to two episodes too long. I think that one I would really just throw in the trash is in Season 2. There's that whole subplot where Chuck goes to a secret sex party and, like, meets the nanny and Sebastian Stan is a member of this evil sex club or whatever. Either do more with it—like, the secret sex club needs to now be an integral part of *Gossip Girl*—or throw it away.

Far be it from me to reject a crazy subplot, but I always felt that the most effective and interesting storylines were the ones that inspired universal emotion for viewers, especially in terms of family and friend relationships. "My favorite moment was, there's an episode where Dorota gets married and it's a very fraught time for Blair and Chuck, and so we have a really lovely scene where Dorota's able to really comfort Blair and in a really maternal way," Szadkowski said. "And I mean, it's that great mix of like maternal and buddy and 'person you can rely on', you know, and so they have a sweet moment where, where Blair kind of is very open about how imperfect things are with Chuck, how she's heartbroken. That's my favorite scene."

See? Even the cast members play favorites.

Gossip Girl may have been largely ignored by the Emmys and Golden Globes, but the cast earned many a surfboard. Here, Chace Crawford, Leighton Meester, Penn Badgley, and Blake Lively attend the 2008 Teen Choice Awards in Los Angeles.

Photo by K Mazur/TCA 2008/WireImage/Getty Images.

The Best and Worst *Gossip Girl* Storylines

The Worst: Serena and Dan's Secret Sibling

Lily and Rufus had a love child way back when they were still a couple, meaning that Serena and Dan, now dating in current times, share a half-sibling, Scott. The writers dragged this story on for two seasons, with Bart Bass being the first to know and Scott sneaking off to New York to befriend all the players *around* the Humphries and Van

Der Woodsens. Right before Lily and Rufus' wedding, they find out Scott is their kid, they're all, "omg, it's really you," everyone bonds, they say visit anytime, and he leaves and never does. So . . . what was the point of all that?

The Best: Nate's Familial Collapse and Addict Dad

Chace Crawford's Nate is way more conflicted a character than he was probably meant to be, thanks to Crawford's better-than-it-had-to-be performance. The greatest example of this is watching Nate wrestle with the fact that he got his embezzling addict father arrested for what he thought was a little snow in his pocket but was really massive charges from the SEC. The drama! The performances! The eyebrow furrowing!

The Worst: Chuck and Elle and the Secret Society

Chuck's Season 2 subplot involved a hooker with a heart of gold and no shopping on Rodeo Drive. Since he couldn't have Blair, he threw all his focus into helping this sex worker escape an elite secret society? I'll give the writers a point for including that this very same secret society comes back later as the ones who helped Bart Bass fake his own death but like, why did we do this?

The Best: The Crew Ganging up on Georgina

Georgina became more of a friend than a foe as the series progressed, but we first met her when she was trying to blackmail Serena and generally ruin lives. Luckily, the Upper East Side Avengers assembled to send Georgina to boot camp, leaving Blair to utter what is arguably her best line in the series: "Haven't you heard? I'm the crazy bitch around here."

The Worst: Dan and Georgina's Faux Baby

It always felt that the writers only figured out Dan would be Gossip Girl at the very end, because this guy is dumb. He can't take any context clues, and he's full of himself and yet very trusting of people who would do him wrong. Georgina had proven to be a liar from the beginning of the series, and yet when she comes to Dan at the end of Season 3 saying she's pregnant and the baby is his, he's like "Bet, come on in." It's everyone around him that pushes to confirm paternity (the baby is not Dan's), and Dan remains a dingus of the highest order.

The Best: Dan Getting Published in *The New Yorker*

This absolutely unrealistic storyline qualified and maintained the absolute writer delulu that a high school junior is a good enough auteur to make it into the most revered, exclusive literary magazine in the world. The most famous writers that you've heard of and read as part of whatever school curriculum you focused on couldn't get into *The New Yorker*, and Dan Humphrey did. As a writer, I give my thanks and salute. We all need something to wish for that will absolutely never, ever happen.

The Worst: Chuck Agreeing to Trade Blair for His Father's Hotel

I never really knew what to think about Chuck's uncle Jack Bass, since he was a rake and slept with high schoolers but also swooped in to save Chuck when he wasn't trying to ruin him. We all contain multitudes? But Chuck offering up the alleged love of his life, so that Jack will hand over control of Bass Industries is a low point, even for these guys.

The Best: The Ponzi Scheme

Come on, you all know Poppy Lifton and Armie Hammer, I mean Gabriel Edwards, were too good to be true! To quote *SNL*'s Stefan, this Season 2 storyline has everything: a gullible Serena, an alleged future cannibal, Rufus losing hundreds of thousands of dollars, and Georgina changing the takedown plan halfway through because she knows hers will work better. Perfection.

The Worst: Lola and Ivy and Carol and Rufus

Gossip Girl made a whole marketing campaign over "OMFG WTF" and that's what I thought about this whole thing. Lily's sister, Carol, hires an actor to pose as Lily's niece so that Carol can get her inheritance, and chaos ensues. Viewers had to deal with roughly 600 twists from Seasons 4 to 6 in this plotline, and one of them had to do with Rufus dating Ivy, his *step niece*. Ivy wasn't necessarily a bad person, but she came out that way after too many tussles with the Van Der Humphries.

The Best: Dan Is Gossip Girl

If you're a fan who decided to rewatch the entire series with the lens of Dan spying on everyone, *Gossip Girl* takes on a much more nefarious tone. Especially when, at the end, everyone was totally cool with their secrets and lies being aired out as fodder for the gnawing, teething masses. (To say that *Gossip Girl* was prescient about the state of the Internet today is an understatement.) But I say that it set up Penn Badgley's turn as Joe Goldberg on Netflix's *You*,

WRITING, RECEPTION, AND RECAPS

making both shows a part of the Gossip Girl Cinematic Universe. When you think about it this way, doesn't it make you feel better? Instead of thinking about how the writers had six seasons to figure it out and threw a Hail Mary trick play in place of a sensical ending?

3

THE FANS

The perfect combination of sexy storylines, beautiful people, and online buzz quickly made *Gossip Girl* a hit, even if the ratings were never top-tier. (But as we have discussed, ratings are not the whole picture when it comes to youth programming, and especially in the mid-2000s when TV technology was basically Stone Age.) If you weren't there paying attention to the buzz around it, *Gossip Girl* seemed like any other show. But the constant replaying of episodes during the 2007 writers' strike coupled with the sexy ads and the growing use of social media chatter led to all-out fandom mania.

"The writers' strike played a role because that allowed The CW to replay the episodes that already aired, [allowing] people to see what they had missed. I think it came at the right time in terms of social media really starting to blossom," TeenDramaWhore journalist and writer Shari Weiss said.

The first thing was Facebook in 2004, but Facebook, that wasn't really a place where you were discussing TV, especially in those beginning years. Twitter started in 2006, and so if you have *Gossip Girl* premiering in 2007, 2008, that kind of rides that first Twitter wave as people discussing things using hashtags, things like that. There was some levels of built-in fanbase from the books, too.

Tyler McCall, journalist and *Gossip Girl* superfan told me,

> I was hooked from the pilot. I loved it so, so much. It was smart, it was sexy. It was funny. . . . Do you remember that you could buy individual episodes on iTunes? I got an iPod Video, I think, either for that Christmas or the Christmas before. And I had the pilot episode and "The Wild Brunch" on my iPod Video so that I always had them with me if I wanted to watch them.

It took some fans a little bit of time to come around. "I tuned in and I was not a fan! Part of me feels really embarrassed about that I was so off the mark and did not see the massive hit and pop culture cornerstone the show was going to become," Weiss joked.

But The CW was super aware of what was starting to go on in homes all across America and how viewers were communicating with both the family and friends they were watching *Gossip Girl* with and the other super fans across the country. "We used an outside research company and went to different markets to sit in living rooms with viewers: Chicago, Atlanta, Denver, Dallas, and New York. We began to see how viewers were talking about the show," Rick Haskins, then The CW's executive vice president of marketing and digital programs, told *The Hollywood Reporter*. "They would text each other about it, even if they were sitting on the same couch. That really was our 'Aha!' moment. We realized we could flip our marketing and talk about this show the way they talked about it."

So, following along here, let's do some more math: hot people + sexy, aspirational stories + new means of communication + cool marketing = ka-boom! This potent combination in teen TV only meant one thing—that the lives of all of the main cast members were about to explode in ways they never thought possible. "When we first started filming, people would walk by and ask, 'What are you filming?' Once we aired, the whole mania started," Leighton Meester, who played Blair, told *The Hollywood Reporter*.

It wasn't long before *Gossip Girl*'s New York City sets were mobbed with fans trying to get a glimpse of their favorite characters. "We were shooting on the Upper East Side one afternoon and must have been outside three all-girl schools. Within an hour, ten girls multiplied to 300. I mean, we weren't the Beatles," Chace Crawford, who played Nate, added. "Ed [Westwick, who played Chuck] and I were crossing Park Avenue and had a ring of girls around us. We got stuck on the median and our make-up people had to fight them off. They were getting their hair pulled and had to throw elbows to get us through."

"These girls, it was funny because they would come to set and they would be dressed in like, the private school uniform.

[We would] shoot on the Upper East Side a lot. And so they would be coming from school . . . and they would be coming in the same little outfits," recalled Zusanna Szadkowski, who played Dorota. "Everybody did their best to accommodate [the fans]. . . . The guys were so charming and like, I always thought it was great because Ed Westwick, for example, was always so sweet. . . . It was fun for me to watch the whole phenomenon."

The attention was thrilling, albeit uncomfortable for some in hindsight. "I think I used to feel like I was fine with it, but looking back on it from a different perspective now, I never really got used to it," Crawford added. "I'm a private person and I don't like being the center of attention."

Frankly, none of the main cast members had a choice on whether they wanted to be the center of attention, because once it was on with *Gossip Girl* fans, it was really on. Multiple cast and crew on the set of *Gossip Girl* have compared the show's fanbase to that of the Beatles in terms of their fervor. *Gossip Girl* hairstylist Jennifer Johnson told *Vanity Fair*, "I had a little S.U.V. at the time and I had it parked out front of our location at the school. There were just so many fans everywhere, and when we wrapped at the end of the day, there were handprints all over my car. It was like the Beatles were inside."

The adult members of the cast found some humor in the *Teen Beat*-era fan frenzy that was overtaking the set. Sam Robards, who played Nate's father, the Captain, recounted to *Vanity Fair* what it was like to shoot scenes with the heartthrobs of the show: "It was a Friday night around midnight, and we were up on Fifth Avenue and 95th Street, and I looked across the street and there were, like, 200 kids with cell phones, and I said to Chace [Crawford], 'Hey buddy, there are 200 kids on a Friday night in the city [here] . . . and they ain't taking my picture.'"

Kelly Rutherford, who played Lily Van Der Woodsen, told the *Behind The Velvet Rope* podcast she was usually too busy tending to her own kids for fans to approach her as they did the other cast members. "I usually had a stroller with me, or was carrying a kid. It was different, so people approached differently," she said. "It was definitely like moms and daughters, they would just be like 'Oh, hi!' It was different than the young kids, but yeah for sure, it was nice. Matthew [Settle, who played Rufus] and I got a lot of that, when we would go out together."

The common refrain from many of the cast and crew is that they were shocked that so many people would want to just show up to set and watch *Gossip Girl* being filmed. Zusanna Szadkowski said,

> I never really got famous, but I got where people who were big fans of this show, you know, got a kick out of being in the world. So if I did get recognized, it was by somebody who really had a passion for [the show.] For me . . . it meant a lot to me because it was like a direct appreciation of, of the work that I cared about so much. I've never been recognized enough that it became annoying.

It's always made my day. I don't know how [the other cast members] all felt about it, but I, I mean, I know that when we would shoot on location, as soon as the show became popular, there were a lot of fans [waiting] because they were young fans. They're extra and enthusiastic. And so we would shoot, and even just walking from the trailer to the set location, if we were on the street, there were so many young fans that we had to have security and everything. Not because they posed any threat or that it was just like, just make a pathway. Watching that for me was crazy.

Journalist Jason Gay wrote *Gossip Girl*'s iconic 2009 *Rolling Stone* cover story, and he got to experience the on-set madness—which had moved to include not just fans but paparazzi—firsthand while doing his interviews and research for the feature. "The outdoor sets were pretty fun, because the fans come out," he wrote after the article had been published.

There were many kids from local private schools, foreign tourists and tons of paparazzi. It's very strange to see a mob of paparazzi photograph Blake [Lively] and Leighton [Meester] in character as they film an outdoor scene. It's as if the reality of the show exists behind two lenses—in real time and TV time. All the actors enjoy the outside stuff because of the fans, too. It's like playing on stage or something. More energy, more excitement and the sense that anything could happen. And sometimes it does. There is no such thing as a closed set in [New York City]!

Nicole Fiscella, who played Izzy, told me about the shift of having a ton of photographers on set.

> In the beginning, it was not really anything was happening. But then after a few of the episodes aired and people started coming to the set and trying to get pictures and screaming and yelling and all of that, that's when I was like, oh, this is actually something, you know. It was mostly fans in the beginning of what I remember, and then it started to become [paparazzi, too] and then you needed to be covered to get to the set. It just started really taking off. It was not anything I expected. I had no idea. I had not been in that situation before, so I just had no idea that that's what it was going to be. Most of the cast hadn't really been in that situation before.

"I had never seen paparazzi before. So like, if I was walking with Leighton [Meester] or something, we [would be] walking down the street . . . and then the paparazzi would be taking pictures," Szadkowski said. "I think everybody handled it with grace and, you know, a show like that has sort of a symbiotic relationship with its audience." Szadkowski admitted, though, that the addition of paparazzi added challenges to the set.

> It made it more difficult to shoot the show itself, the paparazzi sometimes. And I know this happens on, you know, on a lot of shows, but it's like usually they're cooperative and have like a relationship where, you know, they make an understanding and they'll kind of creep around and get some shots, but they stay out of the

way. But sometimes the paparazzi guys would be in the shot or be disruptive or something.

And as the crowds became bigger and bigger, many on set decided they needed to add their own personal security. "I opened up my trailer door to see, literally, on my first day, I think forty paparazzi," Michelle Trachtenberg, who played Georgina, told *Vanity Fair*. "That's when I was like, 'O.K., I need my own bodyguard.'"

"I remember going to the set one day, and this really big guy, about six feet five, comes up to me, and I thought, 'I don't remember a character like that in the script,'" Jessica Szohr, who played Vanessa, told *Rolling Stone*. "And he says, 'I'm your security guard.' I'm like, 'What?' And we turned the corner, and there were hundreds of little girls."

For some, it was jarring. "I was so shocked by it. These twelve-year-old girls hitting on our cast members. I remember one walked up to Penn [Badgley] and was like, 'Hey, you wanna come over to my house later?'" Serena herself, Blake Lively, told *Rolling Stone*. "That was before they were in any of these teen magazines. The guys were like, 'What. Is. Happening?' It was really instantly a whirlwind."

Things really hit a fever pitch when the cast found out that promoters were running bus and walking tours—like the ones already devoted to *Sex and the City* or *Friends*—and using the spots that the cast members hung out as destinations on the route.

THE FANS

Szohr said on her podcast,

> I think I might have had a couple of episodes off, and I went back to LA, and I came back, and a few of us had found a little pub that we would go and have drinks in our little area after work or every once in a while . . . I remember coming back, I'm walking in to meet [the cast], and there were like forty girls with short skirts and heels, and I was like, this is like a little pub that no one knew about.
>
> And I remember hearing that there were these promoters that would take all these girls to the Meatpacking District to go out to the clubs, and they found out that the hot *Gossip Girl* guys were hanging out at this little pub, so they would come in there. I mean, the way the girls were . . . I mean, sometimes we couldn't get through a scene because they were screaming. They were showing up in short skirts in the middle of winter at a pub just to be in the same room, which is wild.

Crawford and Badgley spoke together on Badgley's podcast, *Podcrushed*, about how hard it was to process the fame that came so fast and then just . . . disappeared when the show was over. "I feel like from the day it was aired . . . from that day until it ended, for those six years, it did not stop," Badgley said.

> Every weekend we had a photoshoot, and then every hiatus, we had either a project or some kind of press tour . . . . The greatest struggle I had with *Gossip Girl* was simply that people thought I was like Dan . . . it puts you back in middle school, and you feel [helpless.]

That's why the second I got out of it I was like, "Oh, I need to deal with that."

"When it all sort of ends, I kind of describe it like an athlete getting injured and ending their career instantly. It all gets pulled out from under you . . . your identity is pulled out from under you," Crawford said. "I didn't handle it too well for a while."

There was another big problem for the producers when it came to all the outside attention that *Gossip Girl* garnered while filming on the streets—spoilers! So much of *Gossip Girl* was filmed on location, on the street, in the public. So many fans and paparazzi followed them around. Thus, many storylines were spoiled or second-guessed, so much so that the show ended up filming multiple scenes and endings to throw fans and tabloids alike off the scent.

The show even dealt with its own *Gossip Girl*-esque scandal when scripts were leaking left and right during filming. "Our scripts were ending up online, and we couldn't figure out how," one of the show's producers told *Vanity Fair*.

> We hired a private investigator. We didn't understand what was happening, because everything was getting leaked, every detail. . . . A teenager, I think either [from] Russia or Bulgaria, had hacked one of the writer's emails, and was selling scripts on eBay. But they were underage, so they couldn't be prosecuted. It was a f–king production

nightmare. We would have to "X" out every script. We would have to print on red paper. . . . It was like there was a Gossip Girl in our system.

Frankly, I just wonder how much money that teenager made from selling illicit *Gossip Girl* scripts to mega fans around the world . . .

In any case, a quick influx of fame and people knowing your name would be an adjustment for any actor, but with many of the cast in their late teens and early twenties, they didn't have the toolbox to deal with this sort of fast-rise notoriety, because *Gossip Girl* was the first big project for many.

"You're just kind of doing your job, and as an actor, you don't think, what if the show gets so big, and there's paparazzi, and if you date your co-star everyone's gonna want to know about your relationship, and all the things that come with that," Szohr said on her podcast. "You don't think about that. So when it did hit the way it did, it was shocking because you're happy because people are liking it, but there was a lot that came with that."

"I never had the attention that [the rest of the cast] got to some extent, which, you know, I was always sort of observing that situation," Stan told Michelle Collins on SiriusXM. "But, still, I was in that world, and it was just fascinating to see how popular that show was."

Taylor Momsen, who played Jenny Humphrey, was the youngest and perhaps had the hardest adjustment. "It was always weird for me, being young and suddenly kind of overnight being tabloid famous, which is a different kind of famous where suddenly there are paparazzi outside your house, and they're following you, and they're following me taking my sister to school," she told Penn Badgley on *Podcrushed*.

> It was weird. They would photograph me on set . . . because we filmed in the streets of New York . . . as my character and put it in the tabloids as "Taylor Momsen". . . . Taylor Momsen's wearing this . . . blah blah and that started to really bug me because my identity was getting taken over in a way where people had this perception of me that wasn't me and so I became very hyperaware of how I carried myself. As I started to get older, I think Eric [Daman, the fashion director] understood that, and he so he started to go, "OK well, we'll dress Jenny a little bit more like you . . . we'll blend the two."

Another added complication was the fact that so many of the cast were dating each other while they were on set, so the constantly shifting relationships both on- and off-screen made everything these actors did tabloid fodder.

Lively told *Vanity Fair*,

> At the time, I was wearing the same clothes and doing fashion shoots, and dating the same person that my character was dating— or sometimes that person [Dan] was my brother, you never know

THE FANS

> with Serena—and because of that, what people were projecting onto me was that I was Serena. . . . We look the same, and we acted the same as far as they could tell, because I wasn't doing anything but that show. If [Badgley and I] were photographed walking down the street, they didn't know if it was a paparazzi shot or if it was a shot from the show. . . . At the time, what was heightened was, wow, it all looks similar from the outside, but it's so different on the inside.

Fiscella was happy to have the gift of age and experience during her time on set.

> For me, it was a little bit easier, I think because I was living in New York and being in New York and you know, I had been there for a long time already . . . and because I was a smaller part too, I don't feel as though I was as affected as everybody else until maybe a little bit later. My life honestly didn't change a ton in the beginning. Whenever I wasn't working, I was going out on [modeling] castings or doing modeling jobs or whatever. I was just so comfortable and familiar with New York. I feel like for everybody else, they were also a lot younger than me, right? Like I was 28. Everybody else was, you know, 20/21/19, you know. So I think for them it was like, wow, this entire world just opened up right where they can go anywhere, do anything . . . I took it in stride, I would say.

"It was super fun, like, and it was overwhelming, too, at times, because we were just growing up, and I think you get a lot of young love and a lot of things that kind of are coming at you very quickly and you're just trying to process it," Stan said. "And . . . when we look back now, I think we can all look back and just kind of go like, 'oh, yeah, that was more fun than we were thinking at the time.'"

Speaking of fun, one cannot discount the amount of perks that come with being very young, very hot, and living and working in one of the best cities in the entire world: "New York City was very nice to the *Gossip Girl* crew and cast. Like, if you wanted a reservation, any restaurant, any concert. I think everyone kind of wanted to have their place in the show, whether it was a store or a restaurant," Szohr said. "They were very, very nice to us, and I'm not going to say we took advantage, but we definitely were in our twenties having fun, like oh yeah, we'll try this restaurant. Oh yeah, we'll go see this concert. Oh yeah, we'll go to Brooklyn and go try out this new venue."

Trachtenberg recounted what was probably the best part of the cast becoming quickly famous in the mid-2000s—the complete lack of camera phones or anything that could record you without you knowing. "We barely really had social media or cameras in the beginning, so it was a lot more private to do more fun things without being inhibited by, like, someone taking a video of you uploading it to Instagram and all that stuff," she told Szohr. "It was really more the beginning of that time, and it was great. We had a ton of fun. We would go out as groups, probably cause some sort of ruckus, and I loved it."

Even celebrities wanted to meet them, too. "I remember we would be at events and, like, Keith Richards' daughters wanted to meet [us], and Sylvester Stallone . . . we'd be in rooms and I'd be like, why is Sylvester Stallone walking over? And he'd be like, my daughters are fans," Szohr said on her podcast.

To really put this in perspective, Sebastian Stan, who played Carter Baizen, is a part of the Marvel universe. He plays Bucky Barnes, aka the Winter Soldier, aka a character that has been in multiple movies and has his own franchise around him. Bucky Barnes also had a TV show, too. So we're talking ultra-comic-book-famous. Marvel famous. Movie star famous. International famous. And still, the thing that gets Stan recognized is having been on *Gossip Girl*. "Once in a while, I'm in a coffee shop, standing in line, trying to get an iced Americano, and I'll just hear, 'Carter Baizen' behind me, and I'll just have to slowly turn around, usually amazed that people still remember that character," Stan told *Variety*.

And if having to battle the crowds in New York City was a feat, the cast and crew were shocked at what they found when they filmed parts of Season 4 in Paris.

"We were told to be prepared, like, you're not gonna get the same crowds you get in New York in Paris when you're shooting there because . . . people don't really watch it . . . I have pictures from that shoot," co-creator and producer Josh Schwartz told Szohr. "The biggest crowds the show ever got were the streets of Paris lined out outside of the hotel. That was another instance of, like, more people are watching this show than we are aware of."

Co-creator and producer Stephanie Savage said it particularly affected Chuck Bass himself.

> Ed [Westwick] couldn't leave his hotel. Fortunately, it was I think [the] World Cup and he just sat in his room and watched soccer, but he couldn't leave his hotel. There were, like, girls camped out on the sidewalk. And the French producers that we worked with, they did *The Sopranos*, they did *Sex and the City*, they did *The Tourist* with Johnny Depp and Angelina Jolie, and they were like, "We've never seen crowds like this."

Director Mark Piznarski was even afraid for his life at moments, given the crush of the growing crowds. "When we shot the Season 4 opener in Paris, it was just an unbelievable experience. There was a time when there were so many [fans], everybody told the security people in France, 'We need security,'" he said. "Well, there were so many fans that they started to rush the cast, and we were all huddled up together and shoved up against the wall like at a concert when the people in the pit

THE FANS

get shoved up against the wall and die, you know? It was like that kind of stuff. It was insanity."

The *Gossip Girl* frenzy was now global, with uber-fans in Europe and Asia, too. "I'll never forget, I had someone come in from China to talk to us because the series was the No. 1 downloaded show in China—obviously not legally, but it had created a huge phenomenon," former CW president Dawn Ostroff told *Vanity Fair*.

It's still interesting to me—and a relic of years past, perhaps—that the ratings on *Gossip Girl* were never particularly amazing, and yet The CW let it run for six seasons. *Gossip Girl* premiered right in the beginning of DVRs and TiVo and iTunes and new ways to consume your favorite media, and The CW was patient about the show finding its footing. As Savage told *The Futon Critic*,

> Television habits are just completely different now than they used to be, and The CW, to their credit, has been very smart and very supportive of us in understanding that. When we got our pickup in Season One, we definitely didn't have the ratings to justify that, but they were very in tune to DVR numbers and iTunes and the amount of streaming that was happening online and they took all those factors into consideration when they picked us up.

Today, we have so many streaming and viewing options that, generally speaking, viewership numbers tend to be lower because it's spread much thinner. And still, Netflix will cancel its most-watched show because it's a Tuesday and the wind blew in a weird direction that morning. Networks don't have the stomach to lose any cash or let a show find its audience these days, so that The CW took a chance is still notable.

If one wants to dive into the full kingdom of *Gossip Girl* fans on the internet, one should look no further than the FanForum page for the show that, yes, still exists! It was unofficially "shut down" in June 2014 for new postings, but the entire archive is still there for your perusal. Yes, all 410 pages of posts and commentary, some with 1,000 responses to every prompt or question, all from *Gossip Girl* fans around the world. The most popular page is a discussion page for the series finale, with 82,536 views, and the most replied-to is about Season 2, Episode 12, "It's A Wonderful Lie." This FanForum board was a place where *Gossip Girl* fans could come and discuss their favorite and least favorite relationships, theories, spoilers, fashion questions, and, really, the sky's the limit. There's fan fiction, which, as we learned from *Fifty Shades of Grey*, is a viable way to create and make money these days. There are ninety-three "appreciation threads" about Leighton Meester and Blair Waldorf alone because, why not? In the beginning days of the internet, we didn't have social media to chatter on. These forums were pretty standard in assorted fandoms, and even when Facebook and Twitter became viable means of communication, these dedicated forums served as community spaces for fans to talk not only about *Gossip Girl* but whatever other things they loved. True friendships and lasting relationships were found in these community groups.

And it's not just FanForum that showed *Gossip Girl* the love. Television Without Pity, colloquially known as TWoP, is a now-defunct pop culture forum that highlighted snarky recaps (the unofficial tagline of the site was, "Spare the snark, spoil the networks.") and heavy community commentary from fans and shitposters alike. Interestingly enough, the entire site was created by and for teen TV lovers as a place to discuss *Dawson's Creek*, and then it expanded to fit in everything from *Gossip Girl* and *The West Wing* to a variety of sitcoms and reality shows. The site was purchased by Bravo in 2007 and shut down in 2014—which, Bravo, you've given me *Vanderpump Rules* and *Southern Charm*, but you've also taken so much away in losing TWoP. Tribune Media bought the site in 2016, it was scrapped in 2017, and the archives died in 2021, so the mass of *Gossip Girl* opinions, recaps, comments, theories, spoilers, and appreciation posts there have officially been lost forever. Sigh.

Fortunately, there are dozens if not hundreds of *Gossip Girl* Tumblr accounts, including one lucky fan that nabbed the "gossipgirl" domain, plus millions of posts, reactions, memes, and more on Twitter (again, I'm not calling it X and you can't make me), Instagram, Reddit, Facebook, and TikTok. The number of posts, frankly, is unquantifiable, because as more and more younger viewers discover *Gossip Girl* for the first time, they want to talk about it as much as humanly possible and keep posting and posting and posting. It's like breathing, basically, to declare your opinions about something on the internet. The demographics seem to be firmly women, with Schwartz confirming this to Szohr on her podcast:

> The numbers of that audience, [it was] women between 18 and 34. That's where it really started to pop and do really big numbers, and that was incredibly appealing to advertisers. I think the show just got a whole rocket booster on it when it went to Netflix for a whole other generation, because it is so binge worthy. If you didn't grow up in that time, it's a perfect way of experiencing the mid-2000s in New York.

(I did, and I agree, it is.)

Though it was mostly women tuning in and discussing, I would be remiss to mention that two of the biggest *Gossip Girl* podcasts, *Gossip Guys* and *XOXO, Gossip Kings*, are helmed by men who want to talk about their love of the show. *Gossip Girl* as a show might not have been that inclusive, but the *Gossip Girl* community itself welcomes anyone who wants to talk about headbands, the Upper East Side, and how you absolutely cannot get from DUMBO to the Palace Hotel in 20 minutes. (On a good day, on public transit, it's 35 minutes if the gods are smiling

THE FANS

upon you and there are no problems or delays. You have to transfer, for goodness's sake. A TRANSFER. It's probably closer to 45. Check Google Maps. And don't take an Uber. Unless you want to be in the car for an hour no matter the time of day. Can you tell that, as a New Yorker, the logistics still really bother me?)

And you know what? Even though I get tripped up by the travel planning and some bum storylines on *Gossip Girl*, that doesn't matter. Because, for fans, *Gossip Girl* is less about the facts but the feelings and the fantasy, and that's why it's still so appealing for millions of people around the globe to watch, to speculate, to commentate, and to hit play just one more time.

Gossip Girl producers thought the United States fan base was passionate, but when the show filmed in Paris in 2010, they were struck by the size and voracity of the crowds of screaming French teenagers.

Photo by Marc Piasecki/GC Images/Getty Images.

Gossip Girl's 11 Best Guest Stars

Tyra Banks

Tyra Mail, incoming! Though Banks was only in one episode, playing Serena's friend Ursula Nyquist in Season 3, this *America's Next Top Model* host was always smizing.

Cyndi Lauper

Lauper played herself in a Season 2 cameo at Blair's 18th birthday party, proving girls, even Blair, always want to have fun.

Rachel Bilson

Summer Roberts appears as herself alongside *Gossip Girl* voice Kristen Bell in the series finale, who, FWIW, thinks Bilson can't "play high school" anymore. Ouch.

Rachel Zoe

In Season 4, Zoe got doused in chocolate at one of Blair's big parties.

Alexa Chung

Another fashion insider who played herself! Considering how iconic her fashion was at the time, her Season 6 appearance was not a surprise.

Lady Gaga

The pop star gave all *Gossip Girl* fans a taste of "Bad Romance" in Season 3.

Vera Wang

If you're gonna wear a Vera Wang wedding dress, you get a Vera Wang fitting. And that's what Blair did when she married Louis.

Brittany Snow

This one is kind of cheating, but Snow played Lily Van Der Woodsen's teenage self in that one capsule prequel episode. Still sad that pilot didn't go anywhere.

Clémence Poésy

Do you think Chuck Bass knew he was dating Fleur Delacoeur from *Harry Potter* in Season 4?

Michael Bloomberg

Gossip Girl is a show that transcends politics, as former New York City mayor and current media billionaire Michael Bloomberg appeared in the series finale, declaring he always thought the real Gossip Girl was Dorota.

Tinsley Mortimer

When my loves of Bravo and *Gossip Girl* collide, I sit up straighter and take notice. Like when former *Real Housewives of New York City* cast and forever socialite Tinsley Mortimer was at the Hamptons White Party in Season 2.

4

DIVERSITY AND DOUBLE STANDARDS

According to New York City's official website, 37 percent of New Yorkers were born outside of the city, and more than half of residents speak a language other than English while at home. Per the 2020 United States census, only a third of New York City residents are white. So where the hell are all the people of color in *Gossip Girl*? The general argument on the steps of the Met (or really just the internet) is that *Gossip Girl* takes place on the Upper East Side, within very moneyed, old-school families, and those people, because of colonialism and capitalism and racism, are largely white and WASPy.

This isn't a particularly new argument for shows of the 2000s that take place in and around New York. *Girls*, *Sex and the City*, and *Friends* all faced the same criticism. And frankly, the teen drama genre in general doesn't get high marks when it comes to different faces, races, and ethnicities on their screen—*The O.C.*, *One Tree Hill*, *Dawson's Creek*, *Beverly Hills, 90210*, *90210*, *Pretty Little Liars*, and, well, literally name pretty much any other teen TV show of the time—all were met with accusations of tokenism and not going far enough to make the cast of characters on the screen reflect the reality of the world.

Out of everyone in the main cast, Vanessa Abrams, played by Jessica Szohr, who identifies as Hungarian and one-quarter Black, is the only person of color who gets any real screen time. There were elements of tokenism in Blair's minions, with Nicole Fiscella, a Black woman, playing Isobel Coates, and Nan Zhang, an Asian American woman, playing Kati Farkasi. These two didn't have a whole lot to do in terms of plot lines on *Gossip Girl*. They were mostly there to serve Blair, tell secrets to further story progression, and look good in matching headbands. Later, Nelly Yuki, an Asian American student, played by Yin Chang, would join in the fray and battle Blair. Gina Torres played Vanessa's mom in a few episodes. Tika Sumpter and Michael Boatman played Raina and Russell Thorpe, respectively, a daughter–father duo who arrived to take down the Bass empire. And uh, that was really it? Besides these characters, it was just a sea of white faces and pretty blonde hair.

It's something the producer Josh Safran says he regrets about his time crafting *Gossip Girl*. "When I look back on *Gossip Girl*, the only things I regret were not as much representation for people of color and gay storylines," he told *Vulture*. "Those are the two things I think we probably could have delved into more deeply, but other than that, I only regret things like not showing

Chuck finger Blair and the dildos and other sexual stuff." Well, as long as it's that and not adding more weird sex stuff to TV's worst couple!

And part of this lack of diversity really has to do with what was going on in the world at the time—there was no driving initiative to make any sort of change in casts and writers' rooms, no matter where you were.

Writer Amanda Lasher told me,

> I think it really is a reflection of where we were at the time with hiring. . . . There were a lot of women in that writers' room, but when I was on other shows where I was the only woman. And then on *Gossip Girl* . . . I think there were one or two Black writers. . . . It just wasn't, there wasn't the representation behind the scenes in the way that there is now. And so I just think it is a reflection of the lack of representation that was happening at the time and the evolution that needed to happen. It's disappointing, and hard to be like, "Yeah, I was part of that system." I'm glad for the changes that have happened, and it's wrong that it took so long. . . . It's not that it wasn't thought about [on *Gossip Girl*]. It was just the intentionality that needed to be there that was not there at the time.

In reality, Fiscella wasn't really surprised that she was one of only a few people of color on the set of *Gossip Girl*. "I think that also because I just came into this situation a little bit older, right, like I was 28 years old, and I also was . . . modeling. Also an industry where I was just told, 'We don't need any more Black girls. We need just one or two on our entire board.' So, I was very used to that," she told me.

> It's not like I felt like I was discriminated against. I just very much knew what my place was. Like, I knew that I was just . . . they needed a couple tokens, right? So they got myself and they got Nan [Zhang, who played Kati Farkasi]. And they were just like, we've done what we need to do. And . . . that was the time, right? Like, I don't think that it was meant in any way except for the fact that like it was, it was the time. . . . Now it's very, very different, but I think then there was, you know, a point where people were just not doing that, not thinking about minorities.

Of her time playing Kati, Nan Zhang told *Mochi Magazine* in 2009, "[Kati] was a fun character; I enjoyed every part of it. But I wish they would have portrayed the characters with more dimension."

Yin Chang expanded upon her disappointment in how Nelly Yuki turned into a "stereotype." In 2021, she spoke to *Teen Vogue* about her experiences on the original *Gossip Girl* set:

> The initial character breakdown that I had auditioned for described the character as someone who was, in a gist, "supremely confident," "beautiful," and bright. The audition for this role came at a time when characters specifically written for Asian American women were so few and far between and I was under the impression, via the sides given for Nelly Yuki's first episode, that the role

DIVERSITY AND DOUBLE STANDARDS

had more complexity and nuance than most other auditions I had seen. I was over-the-moon thrilled when I received the call about booking it.

In the days leading up to the shoot, though, things start to change, especially when she was given a pair of glasses to wear on screen. Chang continued:

> A comment was made about production not wanting viewers to think they were replacing me with another Asian actor who was previously on the show. . . . Along with glasses came the change from what originally called for a character that was overachieving and effortlessly "confident" and "sexy," to overachieving and "timid" and "submissive" perpetuating cultural stereotypes of "the model minority" and this age-old isolating idea that "there can only be one" Asian American individual existing in the same world.

In the 2000s, there wasn't a lot of room to discuss the need for representation, dimension, and nuance on set, Chang said, adding,

> When I was working on CW's *Gossip Girl*, it was not a situation or a space where I felt comfortable to raise these concerns, so I instead focused on finding ways to bring as much texture to the character as one possibly could within the strict structure of a TV script through improvisation of character choices in hopes they'd keep them in the final cut.

For all my snark, Safran put his money where his mouth was in terms of building diversity for the *Gossip Girl* reboot, which he helmed. Nelly Yuki came back for a stint on the reboot, and she told *Teen Vogue* that the setting felt way more "inclusive" and welcoming than she felt it did when *Gossip Girl* was on The CW.

Chang said a casting director reached out to her about coming back with a special storyline. "Josh was still developing that episode and figuring out if I'd be interested in coming back, and if so, he'd want to write something special for me and there was discussion of having Nelly Yuki come back as a more serious editor of a well-respected and highly regarded publication," Chang said.

> I was so moved by what they shared, to know that Josh intentionally wanted to weave Nelly Yuki in as part of the storyline and exercising his authority as a showrunner to make space for a more layered portrayal of the character meant the world to me in regards to representation . . . it gave me hope in knowing that there are allies who want to do their part to usher in change.

Safran also made it his mission to add more diversity to the *Gossip Girl* reboot. He hired *Empire* writers JaNeika and JaSheika James as co-executive producers to help shape the stories. In an interview with TeenDramaWhore's Shari Weiss, JaNeika and JaSheika said that even though they could relate with white characters like Joey Potter and Pacey Witter from

Dawson's Creek, it would have been great to have more representation in the shows we all consumed when we were young, and that's how they approached putting together *Gossip Girl 2: Electric Boogaloo*. "There's a part of me that has the affinity for the show and the characters . . . being able to supersede race in terms of our connection . . . the universality of their experiences," JaNeika said. "I can relate to a character like Joey, I can relate to a character like Pacey, you know, despite their whiteness. . . . At the same time, we understand how important representation is, and it sucks growing up as a teenager and not being able to see ourselves in those spaces."

She commented that she had recently read *Billion-Dollar Kiss*, *Dawson's Creek* writer Jeffrey Stepakoff's book about his time writing for teen dramas, and she was disappointed to hear of the "network politics" that can block diversity behind the scenes.

"Just being in the writers' room and knowing what it's like when the writers [lack] racial diversity and they have to write for certain characters, there's a lot of caution that comes to the table," JaSheika said. "There's a lot of fear, there's a lot of caution, there's a lot of . . . we don't want to be this [or that] . . . as opposed to making sure your room makes up what your screen looks like."

"What's really important is for us to, as creatives, really tap into our humanity, as opposed to kind of just separating ourselves in terms of our race. Obviously, we're black women,"

JaNeika added. "It's a part of our culture . . . [and] it's going to be infusing our writing, but I think that sometimes we kind of dismiss the ability of us to connect as human beings, to feel comfortable writing a narrative of a human being who may not be of the same race or culture."

Of their time getting ready for *Gossip Girl*, JaNeika said,

> I give Josh [Safran] a lot of credit, because . . . when we interviewed with him, [diversity] was one of the first things that he told us . . . was going to be different. That's what attracted us to working on this iteration of the show. We're just in a different time. . . . A *Sex and the City* reboot . . . a *Friends* reboot . . . would you really want to sit here and watch these shows without any people of color? Like, it's just not the world that we live in. It doesn't make any sense. The world is diverse. . . . It's important to be reflective of the world.

JaSheika added, joking, "It's not acceptable anymore! [Those showrunners] will get laughed at!"

Of course, any changes always court controversy—there were some that said Safran and company didn't go far enough to discuss larger-scale issues like systemic racism and colorism. This is particularly interesting because Safran told *Entertainment Weekly* there's a big difference in consciousness between then and now. "[On the original] the kids didn't know better. On this version, the kids know. The kids know where their parents' money came from," he said. "They know what their parents did to get there, or maybe they turned a blind eye to it." Seems like it could have been a good experience to dive even deeper into some of these issues, especially with an audience that would have welcomed it.

Another issue that should have been explored more in the original *Gossip Girl*? Any sort of meaningful LGBTQ representation at all. The only main LGBTQ character is Eric Van Der Woodsen, Serena's little brother. "I was disappointed in the gay plotline with Eric because it never went anywhere, and it felt like pandering, but also like scaredy-cat pandering," noted journalist and *Gossip Girl* recapper Chris Rovzar.

Serena comes home from boarding school because Eric attempts suicide. At the end of Season 1, Georgina outs him at the dinner table, Lily freaks out, and Serena worries about his already fragile mental health. Then, Eric gets a boyfriend, Jonathan, in Season 2, but Jonathan gets annoyed with the general amount of scheming Eric, Jenny, and the rest of the *Gossip Girl* gang do and splits with Eric. Eric gets another boyfriend, Eliot, but we don't really get to know a ton about him, and then Eric was basically written out of the show so that Connor Paolo, the actor who played Eric, could star on *Revenge* on ABC. In the reboot, Jonathan makes an appearance and says he's married to Eric, but that is not canon, in my opinion, because the reboot of *Gossip Girl* is so *meh* I can't connect the two series as one.

Eric Van Der Woodsen had a super-rough go on *Gossip Girl*. Lily, though absolutely fabulous and probably really fun at all the 1990s groupie parties she attended, is the least parental of all the *Gossip Girl* parents, and yes, I am including Bart Bass in that list, too. Eric had no stabilizing influences in his life. Serena bailed, he attempted suicide, and his mom just put him in a center rather than asking him a single question about why he tried to kill himself. His dad was already gone. And when he got a "new" dad in the form of Bart Bass, Bart talked Eric out of bringing Jonathan to a party where press would be in attendance, lest he have to explain why his stepson was in a relationship with another man. Bart had always been manipulative when it came to Chuck and even Lily, but keeping Eric in the closet just to maintain his "good" conservative name in the press and to the rest of the rich people on the island of Manhattan is a bridge too far.

Bart gently steered Eric into keeping his sexuality a secret, and I know there would have been many glad to see Eric come out, be supported by his family, and manage that experience for the millions watching every week. Everyone deserves to steer their own coming-out story, and more diversity of experience would have been nice here.

After Eric left *Gossip Girl*, the LGBTQ vacuum was filled by . . . Chuck Bass? In the *Gossip Girl* books, Chuck is bisexual. In the show, Chuck got one same-sex kiss in Season 3 that wasn't driven by his sexuality but just as a part of one of his and Blair's many annoying games. Safran defended this choice to *BuddyTV*, saying,

> Chuck is not bisexual in the first book. The pilot mirrors the first book, and [creators] Josh [Schwartz] and Stephanie [Savage] drew from there for each character. We've deviated from the books for the show quite a bit, but it's important to state that there was never a "we don't want to make Chuck bisexual" conversation. The book was used merely as the launching point for the character of Chuck, for each character. Once the show was up and running, the writers' room mindset, per Josh and Stephanie, was to "let the books be the books and let's use them where we can, but let's also make the series the series."

Safran maintained that Chuck's same-sex kiss was created "organically" for the story, adding that it was not a stunt. "It's a great episode filled with so many juicy things. It's not like we were sitting there pitching promos like 'You'll never believe what Chuck's about to do!', and again, when you see the episode, you will see it's not that kind of moment. It's truly a tiny character beat in a much larger story," he said.

"I'm proud of how we've woven gay characters into the tapestry of the show. I feel like, as the only gay writer on the show from the beginning and as someone who feels a huge responsibility towards the creation of fully realized gay characters in television, I am supremely proud of what *Gossip Girl* has done with its gay characters," Safran said.

If you look at Eric, in my mind, he is in one of the only, if not the only, secure relationship on the show. He is also one of the youngest out gay males on network television. And starting with Georgina's outing of Eric, we've done, in my opinion, really strong stuff surrounding the reality of being a gay teenager, that how for some people in your world it's not a big deal, but for other people, they might try to use it against you, hurt you for it. It's never black and white, and it's never easy.

Also not easy was listening to the way the public treated the women on the show versus the men: the double standard that never, ever goes away. The 2000s were an absolutely rough time to be a woman, because it was bad to be a feminist but also there was no need to be a feminist because women could do anything men did but also you couldn't call out misbehavior because what are you, a narc? There were a ton of rumors that circulated around the *Gossip Girl* set that Leighton Meester, who played Blair, and Blake Lively, who played Serena, didn't get along with each other. Serena and Blair were best friends that fought over men and had fundamental personality differences, and yet they still were there for each other on a most foundational basis. But these were characters, not real people—so why did this tit-for-tat infighting have to extend to the actors? This was literally a job for them. It wasn't even real life.

The *New York Daily News* even posted a blind item during the run of *Gossip Girl* reading, "Which rival young actresses on the same hit show are forced to pose together at PR events, even though they hate each other? One resents the other for having knocked her off her 'star of the show' pedestal." The two tried to shoot down these rumors every chance they got. "Honestly, every interview, someone asks me, 'Are you really friends with Blake?'" Leighton Meester told *Rolling Stone* in 2009. "No, of course you're not friends with Blake," Blake Lively added.

Lively also noted that these kinds of rumors didn't happen with the men on the show. "You never hear that Ed [Westwick] and Penn [Badgley] are jealous of each other, even though they are complete frenemies," she said at the time. Crawford and Westwick lived together and worked together, and the media encouraged a bromance story, highlighting just how chummy these two guys were. There were also a few gay rumors here and there, which were quickly shot down, lest they ruin the vibe of Nate and Chuck on the show. (For the record, Crawford and Westwick both identify as straight in their personal lives.) Hello, sexism! Has anything changed?

According to Weiss, that's a big old no: "There were all kinds of rumors that Leighton and Blake Lively did not get along on set. And these rumors largely evaded the men . . . there's a level of stereotypes involved. There's a level of misogyny involved," she told me.

> [Even today], Jessica Szohr [who played Vanessa] got married, and there were headlines like, "Blake Lively wasn't at Jessica's wedding!"

> You know who else wasn't there? Leighton and Taylor and the other people [from the show]. It's still happening [today], which is nuts. It's like we haven't learned the lessons . . . I don't necessarily feel that we've really moved on that much in the culture.

Suffice to say that all of these people worked together. Did you have all of your coworkers at your wedding? Would you? I didn't.

In 2017, Safran told *Vanity Fair* that of course the leading ladies of *Gossip Girl* were not BFFs but instead cordial coworkers. "Blake and Leighton were not friends. They were friendly, but they were not friends like Serena and Blair," he said at the time. "Yet the second they'd be on set together, it's as if they were."

Michelle Trachtenberg, who played Georgina, also insisted that the rumors were just sexist drivel. "It's funny," Trachtenberg said, "Because when we were filming, there was, 'Leighton hates Blake, Blake hates Leighton, everyone hates Blake, everyone hates Leighton . . .,' and blah, blah, blah. It really wasn't. We were all chill. It was cool."

Cool or not, here's a thought: The media certainly took up the idea that Meester and Lively hated each other, but did the show do anything to halt it? Or maybe did they just . . . lean into it? From the sound of it, it was the latter. Meester and Lively played different characters and were different people with different approaches to growing their fame and careers. Why was this revolutionary, and why did it lead to such polarity? A lot of the interviews that the producers did while the show was airing very much highlighted the differences between the two women. And I get that, wanting eyeballs and wanting the zeitgeist to follow you around—but at what cost? Amplifying to young women that you can't trust your friends? That all female friendships are competitive, and no women can simply get along with each other? As a young woman, I had this attitude that men made better friends because they weren't as "dramatic" as women were, but that's not true. That's because I grew up in a culture that made it seem like it wasn't possible for women to have truly supportive, close relationships. Today, my female friendships are my lifeline, my heart, my way to make sense out of an insane world, and it's a shame that potentially *Gossip Girl* wanted to overlook this in order to get eyeballs on the TVs. But, then again, it was just another part of growing up as a woman in the 2000s (And 1990s. And 1980s. And . . .).

Here's an example of what I'm talking about. "Blake is very much in the moment. Blake knows what's happening. She knows this movie's coming out, this band is happening. You talk to Blake on a very contemporary level, and she would be like, 'I'm doing this thing tonight. Have you been to this restaurant?'" Safran told *Vanity Fair*. "Leighton was very removed and very quiet, and, after her scenes were done, she would wander the stage. I had this image of her just in these gorgeous dresses with a book in her hand, sort of a little bit out of focus out in the corners." It's a dichotomy. Blake Lively is fun and pretty and out there and in the know, and Leighton Meester just wants to go home. What a killjoy!

In that same interview, Schwartz and Savage also highlighted the differences in how both women could be perceived by the public based on what their characters would be like.

"It was funny," Schwartz said, "When we first started talking to Blake, it was like, in order for this show to work and for you to be the ultimate New Yorker, you're going to have to host Saturday Night Live and be in a Woody Allen movie." (Note: the Woody Allen thing didn't age well, huh?) Later, Schwartz added, the fact that Lively was on the cover of *Vogue w*as "Blair's nightmare."

Writer and producer Amanda Lasher told me that the competitive nature of the characters was just simply female friendship. "We all felt very strongly, very strongly, that these two were ride-or-dies forever and that they were the true, that they were the love story of the show. And that it was . . . really a realistic depiction of female friendship. It was genuine friendship and that they really were there for each other and that that was very important," Lasher said. "And I do think that there was truth to things and that like, there are power imbalances in female friendship. And there is something to be said about that and to write about it."

Schwartz and Savage spoke to Szohr about Serena and Blair highlighting the "complexities" of female friendships, with Schwartz noting that there was an idea that "your best friend could also be your worst enemy." While it's true that friend relationships have as much complexity as romantic relationships, it does women everywhere a disservice to think that competition always has to happen.

Gossip Girl made so many strides in terms of pushing the envelope on what television could do and what the right marketing could do for network TV, but clearly, through a modern lens, there was plenty more the show could have achieved in terms diversity, equity, and equality.

Lasher agrees. "I come from comedy, and the misogyny in that world was off the charts. And so when I switched over to drama, I was like, wow, progressive. Obviously, I look back now on some of the things that I wrote or said or like, or a trans joke that may have made it into something," she told me. "And I'm like, 'Oh my God,' you know? And I guess all I can do is just be grateful for the evolution . . . to have daughters and look back on that and realize some of the things that we normalized that we [shouldn't have]."

Blake Lively and Leighton Meester appear on MTV's *Total Request Live* in 2007. Photo by Scott Gries/Getty Images.

The Meme that Got Us Through a Pandemic: Go Piss Girl

Cultural moments require extrapolation. Once an idea is out there in the world, it's up to whoever wants it to make it their own—all art is basically just a tweak of another piece of art, and so on and so forth. And isn't great art made in times of stress, upheaval, and struggle?

Picture it: it's April 2020. The world is in what we now know is the beginning stages of the coronavirus pandemic. Lockdowns abound. Fear and uncertainty are high. And

DIVERSITY AND DOUBLE STANDARDS

since everyone is at home with not much to do except watch TV, people started streaming *Gossip Girl* again in earnest, leading to what is possibly one of the greatest memes of all time.

The image that started it all, thanks to an intrepid internet user. The "Go Piss Girl" meme was created in 2020 and spawned many, many spinoffs.

Photo by James Devaney/WireImage/Getty Images.

On a meme-related Facebook group, Tyler Wood took a little bit of ingenuity and some photo editing software, a bit of boredom and a lot of ridiculousness, and made true art—it's an image of Serena saying "I have to pee" and the *Gossip Girl* title letters rearranged to have Blair say "Go piss girl." Simple. Effective. It's so emblematic of a time. You didn't need a back story or even a particular sense of humor to giggle along with "Go Piss Girl." You just needed to be stuck at home or at work as necessary personnel and have an internet connection. How many hours did I lose on social media during 2020? None, really, because I cherished them all. I had "Go Piss Girl" and its many, many inspired iterations, to keep me laughing during a bad, fucked-up time.

5

SEX, LIES, AND *GOSSIP GIRL*

A book about *Gossip Girl* would be remiss if it didn't mention all of the sexy, racy fun the characters were allegedly having. (Though this elder millennial is now exhausted at the thought because she goes to bed at 8:30 p.m. in pajamas that Dick Van Dyke would wear on his 1950s sitcom.) Every generation thinks the generations that come after are particularly off the rails, because that's what happens when you hit a certain age and you don't want to have to find a new jean shape to get comfortable in (see again millennials and their skinny silhouettes). Adults were horrified in the 1950s when Elvis became famous for—clutch your pearls—gyrating his pelvis on television. In the 1960s, the free love, counterculture, Woodstock-adjacent movement sent every Donna Reed holdover reaching for the smelling salts. Disco, Andy Warhol, Marilyn Minter, Ozzy Osbourne, Madonna, Tupac, *Saturday Night Live*, Marilyn Manson, Prince, David Bowie, 2 Live Crew, *My So-Called Life*, George

Michael—all popular acts of artistry that had the Tipper Gores of the planet screaming "What is this world coming to?"

Suffice it to say that teen dramas have always had a certain amount of parental hand wringing and controversy surrounding the idea of hormonally hopped-up teenagers doing what their bodies are telling them to do, but, looking back, what's compelling (and problematic, too, since we are allowed to contain multitudes) about *Gossip Girl* is that the sex was built in from the beginning. The introduction to the sexuality of the *Gossip Girl* characters happens *in media res*, as part of the reason Serena left town in the first place was because she slept with Nate, her best friend's boyfriend, on a hotel bar during a wedding. The sex scene is pretty chaste compared to what we see today, just lots of soft lighting and panning cameras, but what's different is Serena is already devirginized when we meet her. On *90210*, *The O.C.*, *One Tree Hill*, and others, the main character—which Serena is on *Gossip Girl*—frets over the moral and mental consequences of having sex to complete the "should you be having sex right now!" plot line. That doesn't happen quite in that way here.

It doesn't mean that there is no morality or hand-wringing when it comes to sex on the show. Watching it in 2007, I was always struck by how cool and sexy it all seemed, mostly because I was approximately the same age and no one was doing *anything* like what these kids were doing on TV. So I'm not going to say it was aspirational, but it was fun and sexy and made viewers want to watch more. But now, fifteen years later, as a married adult woman who has been watching years of #MeToo and reexamining the events of my own life, I can't help but look at the sex on *Gossip Girl* through a lens of "ick," "eesh," and ". . . that was a choice."

Let's jump in with Serena Van Der Woodsen, the star of the show, the sun which the first season orbits around. When Serena comes back to Manhattan from her Connecticut boarding school, it seems she is less worried about her sexual past than, well, everyone around her. She is slut-shamed from basically every angle throughout the entire series, whether it's Chuck trying to goad her into sleeping with him or Lily, Serena's own mother, saying, "I always knew you had a wild side, but how can you look at yourself? What have you become?" when she thinks her daughter filmed a sex tape. In truth, that video is the one that has Pete Fairman—a much older man, for what it's worth—overdosing, which was one of the reasons why a terrified Serena left Manhattan in the first place. Lily immediately jumps to conclusions because of Serena's allegedly checkered past when all Serena needed was help and, I don't know, parenting (?). Not a lecture.

There's one particular exchange in Season 3 between Nate and Serena that sums up everyone's attitude toward Serena. Jenny Humphrey has decided to lose her virginity to Damien Dalgaard, and Nate doesn't think she should, insinuating that for some girls—who are *not* like Serena—losing one's virginity should mean something more. Serena takes umbrage with this, which, I would, too, and Nate responds back with a list of men Serena allegedly slept with. When Serena says those guys took liberties with their stories or they told all-out lies, Nate throws it back in Serena's face that he lost her virginity to her in the Campbell Apartment at the Shepherd wedding. Serena's response? "And somehow that reflects poorly on me and not you? Talk about a double standard," she says. Tell them, Serena, because this is a tale as old as time.

The Season 1 Thanksgiving episode, "Blair Waldorf Must Pie," flashbacks to the Thanksgiving before, and Serena is a drunk mess stumbling through the streets of Soho. She is wearing a leopard print. (The universal pattern of tramps and mob wives and girls like me from Long Island. I wear it proudly.) The song "Promiscuous" by Nelly Furtado is literally the soundtrack to her scene. Could we be any more heavy-handed with the allusions to Serena's sexual past? And the funny thing is, in Season 5, we learn Serena became a sex object in the tabloids prior to Season 1 because she was wearing a white dress that got wet, and some paparazzi took a picture of it and blasted it out to the world. She didn't pose for it. She had to have been, what, all of 14 years old?

It really bothers me that this is a girl who is never, ever given the benefit of the doubt. All of the other characters on the show have sex, sometimes in weirder or more morally repugnant situations than Serena has ever gotten herself into, but Serena is always the one who is blamed. Blair needs a pregnancy test when she sleeps with Nate and Chuck, and Serena is the one photographed buying it. Because, duh, of course *she's* the one who could be pregnant. Over the course of the series, Gossip Girl blasts that Serena bought a pregnancy test and that Serena has an STD, and people believe both. Nate and Dan go and get tested for STDs after that blast because, even though Serena has wizened and changed considerably as a person from the show's first scenes, they don't trust that she actually has, even though she begs and pleads them not to give in to the rumors because they're not true. She's accused of trying to trade sex for good grades in college. She is targeted by her alleged friends, and Juliet drugs her, after which Lily checks Serena into the Ostroff Center because she's convinced Serena went on a bender. No wonder why Blake Lively famously doesn't drink—her time spent playing Serena showed her all the ways it can go wrong for you if you do or people *think* you do. Serena has low self-esteem and is constantly seeking validation because no one has ever validated her for anything other than her looks. She doesn't need rehab or an attitude adjustment—she needs a friend.

Let's go back to Lily for a second, because she is the queen of not giving her daughter the benefit of the doubt when in reality, this behavior is something Lily caused. In Season 4, Lily makes an offhand remark about Serena never being a "kid"—which, what is that old adage about our parents being our first bullies? Why do you think she was never able to be a child, *Lily?* Lily also tells Serena that she doesn't have boyfriends—instead, she builds "life rafts" to save herself. Serena counters that Lily is actually the one that builds rafts and leaves her children to proverbially drown. She marries whatever rich man comes through and mostly abandons her children to live in the glow of her new love story. Serena was known as a party girl before Pete and boarding school, so she was 15 when she got her "reputation" around town, cavorting with grown men. Um, Lily, which husband were you on while you let the city's socialite scene sexualize your daughter? Lily's neglect and Serena's father William's absence made it possible for Serena to seek validation in other places that weren't healthy for her. This is the same girl who mentioned that one of Lily's boyfriends taught her gambling strategy using candy, and that another of Lily's men used to leave cocaine all over the house. This is especially funny because Lily was known to have been a party girl herself—Rufus always says he could tell the stories about finding her on tour buses with guys like Nine Inch Nails frontman Trent Reznor.

Serena has a series of inappropriate relationships with older men. There's no question of that. Her teacher, Ben, didn't sleep with her but took too much of an interest in her, so much that Lily had him thrown in jail. Tripp Van Der Bilt seduced Serena, and he was married. Colin was her professor. Gabriel scammed her. And Aaron Rose . . . well, he was just really annoying. But he did treat Serena as a muse, solely as an object, rather than a fully formed human being. Serena was under the age of consent for so many of these relationships that I have to once again say,

Lily, were you planning on parenting or just attending charity balls and luncheons? The relationships were inappropriate, but I can certainly understand Serena feeling like she had to find love someplace else other than her own home.

From Serena, to her best friend Blair. Season 1 also opens with Blair deciding to "give" her virginity to Nate, who she has been with for years, mostly as a way to keep him from running back to Serena after Serena returns to Manhattan from her Connecticut boarding school following her brother Eric's suicide attempt. Yes, these are sentences that one could only write when talking about a show like *Gossip Girl*. We come into Blair's non-contemplation of her virginity as it's happening at her mother's dinner party, and she has no moral quandaries or misgivings in the vein of that famous line from *Mean Girls*, "don't have sex, you will get pregnant and die." Blair's sexuality is more of a defense mechanism than anything else, which, though not the right reason to have sex, is seemingly better than wondering what she'll be branded if she decides to have sex. As viewers dive into the first few episodes of Season 1, Blair has more opinions about the La Perla lingerie she'll wear when she and Nate do the deed than about the actual sex itself. But after Blair learns about Nate's infidelity and forbids him to see Serena, and Nate, attending the masked ball, tells Jenny, who he thinks is Serena, that he still has feelings for her (Serena, that is, who as we have discussed, is a dirty skank), Blair decides she's had enough of being whatever good girl the world thinks she is. She drops her clothes, tastefully, of course, this is Blair we're talking about, on Chuck's burlesque stage and loses her V-card to Chuck, of all people, in the back of his limo.

Three episodes later, Blair and Nate finally do the deed, with Nate thinking it's her first time until three episodes after that, when both guys slut-shame her for sleeping with both of them, with Chuck saying, "You held a certain fascination when you were beautiful, delicate, and untouched. But now you're like one of the Arabians my father used to own: Rode hard and put away wet." A horse comparison. Charming. One pregnancy scare later, which Serena took the fall for, Chuck and Blair are a thing, and they remain that way, on and off, throughout the course of the entire series. The only person who slut-shames Blair is Chuck, for the record.

You didn't think we were going to get through *Gossip Girl* without a teenage pregnancy scare, did you? They happen in every teen drama, without fail. These morality lessons were usually geared toward the female characters because under the patriarchy, if you're a woman and enjoy sex, it makes you a wanton slut who should be punished. I'm not saying that anyone should begin their sexual lives without feeling ready and confident in their decisions, but the prevailing TV notion of "Oh my god, is this the right thing? Am I wrong for having tingling feelings in my special parts? We used ten forms of birth control but I am probably pregnant, right?" is frankly, exhausting.

Jenny's first sexual encounter on the show is when Chuck tries to rape her on the roof of the Kiss on the Lips party in the pilot. She then loses her virginity to Chuck a few seasons later, and the audience is supposed to wipe the first episode from our collective memories. (And then Gossip Girl, aka Dan, announces that his sister and Chuck did the deed. Mmmkay, normal.) When Rufus and Lily get married, Jenny is supposed to live with Chuck, her stepbrother, the guy who attempted to rape her at a party. Are we seeing how none of the parents offer any protection here? Fourteen-year-old-ish Jenny is also hanging out with her model friend, Agnes, and Agnes's older boyfriend, Max, in Season 2 when Agnes prods Jenny to remove her clothes and dance while Max takes pictures of them for the fashion line. Is this a Terry Richardson allusion or something? An indie sleaze Cobrasnake throwback? Jenny and Agnes are minors, so this is a literal federal crime. Jenny is very much underage here, so even though she was OK with these photos being taken, she's too young to consent anyway! When Jenny wanted to lose her virginity to Damien Dalgaard, everyone had an opinion on what she could do with her own body, even though it was none of their business.

There are two problematic lenses that define many of the sexual relationships on *Gossip Girl*: that of a distinct age differential, which, if someone is a minor, cannot be consensual, or that of a "let's just sweep it under the rug" approach. Let's take a look at the first one. If Serena is about 17 when she comes back to Manhattan, it means she was about 16 when she ran away to boarding school after Pete died. Georgina mentions that Pete is in his twenties when he is hanging out with high schoolers, making him a—say it with me now—predator. *Gossip Girl* didn't do enough to name the predators as they popped up, so that's what I'll be doing here! The only reason Pete died was because he tried to sleep with Serena, again, a child at the time, and when she rebuffed his advances, he decided to snort a line of cocaine, and then he had a seizure. Good riddance, I say. There are all sorts of disgusting people (mostly men, sorry) on the internet that are still convinced that a female minor can consent to whatever Pete was trying to get Serena to do, and to them I say, "Eat glass."

As for the "nothing to see here" view, Chuck Bass attempts to sexually assault multiple women over the course of the entire series, and we are supposed to forget about it. See: Jenny Humphrey and Serena Van Der Woodsen, who had to physically fight Chuck away in the hotel kitchen in the first episode of the series. He sells Blair, the woman he is supposed to love, to his uncle, Jack Bass, in return for control of the family business, and when Blair says she'll go through with it because she loves Chuck, Chuck is all, that's your choice. If you want even more of the problems with Chuck and Blair, skip over to the next chapter—this paragraph is just the tip of the iceberg. This all said, it's not just the women on the show who are sexualized in inappropriate ways. Chuck is hypersexualized, as well. He lost his virginity to Georgina when he was like, 13 years old, but it certainly doesn't give him the right to act the way that he does when it comes to sex and women, especially women he claims to love.

When it comes to Gossip Girl himself, Dan, the story is just as complicated. Serena tries to break up Dair (that's Dan and Blair, a pairing that never made any sense to anyone, ever) by seducing Dan in the Campbell Apartment in Season 5. She secretly films their sexual encounter, which is revenge porn. Dan did not give consent to their rendezvous, but I suspect this recording and trickery was easier to stomach because it was Serena recording Dan and not Dan recording Serena. (Though, by the end, when Dan is Gossip Girl, we might think all the stuff he does to the rest of the group is just as bad, especially since Serena didn't put this sex tape on the internet for everyone to see?) Dan starts the series as a virgin and feels inadequate before his first time with Serena in Season 1, but the moment ends up being really sweet and touching—a good example of what losing your virginity should be like, and not a circus or mental game like the rest of them. But in Season 2, Dan lies about sleeping with multiple women he's dating while he's doing his book thing, and then he sleeps with Rachel Carr, who is, again, a teacher at his school. (*Pretty Little Liars* had to take their playbook directly from *Gossip Girl*.) This whole "they're a minor" thing isn't limited to the women of *Gossip Girl*—Rachel Carr is an adult, and Dan is not. There's no room for interpretation there. Dan is also a part of the world's most boring threesome. I have more problems with his being Gossip Girl, which means he was unrelentingly spying on all of his friends and loved ones to further his own ambition, which is icky and gross in a different way.

Nate loses his virginity to Serena in Season 1, and then in Season 2, enters into a sexual relationship with Catherine, a woman who is two decades his senior. Again, he is just of age or under it, since this is their second season, and Catherine is an adult woman. A grown-ass lady. No one blinks an eye at it, probably because she's rich? I dunno. It matters that she is married, but not that this is a statutorily illegal relationship. In Season 5, Nate may be legal, but he engages in another large-age-gap sexual relationship with Diana Payne, also at least in her forties. Nate dates many more women on *Gossip Girl*, most of whom are in an acceptable age bracket for him, but it's worth noting that his last relationship in the series is with Sage Spence—a teenager at the time. The student becomes the master, and truly, what the fuck, *Gossip Girl*?

When it comes to sex on TV, *Gossip Girl* paved the way for shows like *Euphoria* to go from 0 to 60 with nudity and sexual situations. In fact, it feels a little quaint to be complaining about the sexual storylines on *Gossip Girl* when there is nearly constant nudity and graphic sex in today's content. But there are key differences here. Firstly, there's a big discrepancy between what you can show on network TV versus cable—*Euphoria* is on HBO, where anything goes, including excessive nudity—and secondly, most of the sexual encounters in *Euphoria* are not exactly portrayed in a flattering light. If anything, *Euphoria* highlights the impulsiveness of teenage hormones and the regret and comedown after the encounter. A lot of the sex on the show has consequences. Neither *Gossip Girl* nor *Euphoria* portray good, everyday sex as it should be—ideas of consent, boundaries, and protective measures pretty much go out the window—but *Gossip Girl*'s glossy finish (*Euphoria* is much bleaker as far as teen dramas go) never explores the problematic elements of the sex its characters are having. It only talks about the sex it thinks certain characters are having (hello, Serena) and condemns said characters through that.

Gossip Girl's sex-forward vibe continued offscreen, as well. I know it was the 2000s, where we were supposed to all be feminists but you were labeled a hag or a harpy or a killjoy if you questioned any offensive joke, but the most famous photoshoot of the series was Leighton Meester and Blake Lively sharing a dripping, messy ice cream cone on the cover of *Rolling Stone*. Inside the magazine, one could find Meester and Lively sharing a piece of licorice à la *Lady and the Tramp*, and a shot with Lively's thumb in Meester's mouth. The whole cast is half-dressed in bed in another photo from the shoot, and don't forget the pillow fight! The whole feature was lensed by photographer Terry Richardson, who has had multiple allegations of sexual assault filed against him since 2017 . . . the most recent was in 2023. The sexuality of the shoot, nay, all the press, though, was the point—these actors were young and hot, and they were all dating each other, too. It was hard to see where *Gossip Girl* ended and the actors' personal lives began, and it was made to feel that way.

Lively and Badgley dated on screen and in real life for the first four seasons of *Gossip Girl*. Ed Westwick and Jessica Szohr dated. Meester and Sebastian Stan dated. Chace Crawford admitted to Alex Cooper on *Call Her Daddy* that he had hooked up with various co-stars, though he declined to say who.

It doesn't seem strange to me that these actors should date—if you're on a set working for 12–14 hours a day, who else are you going to meet? Your work is your life when you're on a television show. But according to Lively, there was a point when all those lines blurred.

"I remember there was one point where we were just afraid of how our personal lives overlapping our work life could be perceived by our bosses. [But then] we were like, 'Oh no, that's exactly what they want,'" she told *Vanity Fair*. "They wanted us all to date. They wanted us all to wear the same clothes that we're wearing on the show. They wanted that, because then it fed their whole narrative. People could buy into this world."

Badgley agreed with his ex-girlfriend. "It really does feel like we're living the show sometimes," he told *Vulture*. "The psychology of celebrity is such a weird and new thing. I think the last time people treated anybody else like this was demigods like in the time of ancient Greece."

Still, credit must be given where it's due when it comes to the boundaries that *Gossip Girl* pushed when it came to sexuality on television and the recognition of how different it is today. Producer and writer Amanda Lasher recounted to Jessica Szohr on her podcast just how much has changed in writing a sex scene then and a sex scene now:

> In terms of writing a sex scene, sometimes it's super fun and you can really get into what you want it to be, and then other times it does become kind of technical, depending on how you shoot it. . . . It's really changed now . . . before . . . there would be playfulness in the writing, and there would be . . . a little bit of freedom for the director in terms of how far we wanted to take it.
>
> But it would depend on what the sex scene is, because sometimes like the sex scene is just about like, they're off kissing and you know, they fall to the bed and we know what's going to happen. But other times, you are telling a story that . . . the sex is very important, and so then you need to make sure that that's in the writing and then that's really clear.

Even in the before times of 2007, though, Lasher had a huge win on *Gossip Girl* in writing and getting a female masturbation scene on network television well before the "watershed hour" of 10:00 p.m.—now that, my friends, is groundbreaking, even today. Portrayals of female desire and female sexuality not through the male gaze are growing in numbers today, but in 2007, it was basically—hold on, let me count . . . zero.

"It is still one of my proudest moments as a writer. I was like, Blair is going to masturbate. That's what's going to happen because she is thinking about [Chuck] and that's what she would be doing. And I remember when I pitched it in the room, people signed off on it," she said. "[Co-creator] Stephanie [Savage] was on board, everyone [was on] board. But I remember being really, really nervous when we got notes from the studio . . . [and they] just skipped right past it."

Know who wasn't happy? A conservative advocacy group called the Parents Television Council. They didn't agree with much of anything that *Gossip Girl* did, even calling the series "mind-blowingly inappropriate," which *Gossip Girl* used in their ad campaign for Season 2. My thing is, if you don't want your children to watch the sexy *Gossip Girl* storylines, don't let them watch *Gossip Girl*. But perhaps some parents want to parent as little as Lily Van Der Woodsen, amirite?

The Parents Television Council also hit the roof when it came to *Gossip Girl*'s highly publicized threesome between Dan, Vanessa, and guest star Hilary Duff, who played actress Olivia Burke. *Gossip Girl* teased this thing out for what felt like a whole season, and the general reaction following the episode was that of disappointment. (So in that way, it was probably the realest sex act performed on the show.) Truthfully, I'm not sure what viewers expected a threesome before 10:00 p.m. on a network teen drama to look like, but it was never going to be anything other than what it was. It worked for ratings though, with a 20 percent gain in viewership from the previous week, per Nielsen. It was the most-watched Monday of the season for The CW, because when in doubt, a good gimmick draws plenty of eyeballs.

Some sexy times that didn't make the cut on *Gossip Girl*? "We had a story about Chuck taking care of Blair under a table at Xan's," producer Josh Safran told *Vulture* as *Gossip Girl* aired its last episodes. "I don't think we were able to do it, but we hinted at it." There were also talks of Georgina further tormenting Serena by sending her a huge box of dildos and other sex toys. "There were dildos she sent to Dan at the house, and we had these really huge dildos in this house that Penn [Badgley] was so shocked to see—but we cut it because you couldn't show them on air," said Safran. "The deleted-scene version, which I don't think we ever put anywhere, is hilarious because they're like a foot and a half long. Penn was really shocked."

I'm not sure either of these deleted racy moments would fly on network TV today either, but it just goes to show—forward movement and progressiveness are in the eye of the beholder. In 2007, *Gossip Girl* was seen as particularly groundbreaking in the way they treated sex, but with a 2020s lens, we can see that a lot of it was the same old same old attitudes and pressure we've all been watching for years.

Chace Crawford and Ed Westwick during downtime on set. The on-screen best friends were also famously roommates in New York City's Chelsea neighborhood during much of filming.

Photo by James Devaney/WireImage/Getty Images.

Serena Van Der Woodsen Is the Manic Pixie Dream Girl of the Upper East Side and It Sucks

In 2007, writer Nathan Rabin coined the term "manic pixie dream girl" (we will call her "MPDG" for short hereafter; it's worth noting that Rabin wrote an entire article for Salon.com in 2014 apologizing for inventing the phrase) in response to Kirsten Dunst's character in *Elizabethtown*, a largely forgettable Cameron Crowe movie with an excellent soundtrack. Per Rabin, the MPDG is a figure who "exists solely in the fevered imaginations of sensitive writer-directors to teach broodingly soulful young men to embrace life and its infinite mysteries and adventures." See also: Natalie Portman's character in *Garden State*, Zooey Deschanel's character in *New Girl*, Zooey Deschanel's character in *(500) Days of Summer*, and Zooey Deschanel's character in basically anything else. It's a young, quirky, always beautiful woman who walks to the beat of her own drum and serves as a muse for a sad-sack young man. She's young and beautiful and free and wild and has perhaps a dark secret or two that we don't hear about because that's too complicated. She's never that complex—she's just a mirror for a man to figure out his feelings against—and she's normally found in quirky indie shows.

Gossip Girl was as mainstream and commercial as it gets, with primetime placement on a major teen network and six seasons of soap opera-style storytelling, but, like many shows and films in the late 2000s, it was unable to escape the siren call of the MPDG in its writers room. Enter Serena Van Der Woodsen.

Now, some of you might be reading along saying, Nah, she gives off main-character energy more so than anyone else on *Gossip Girl*. To that I would say, Wrong—I know Serena is at least a Leo Rising given her hair (her birthday is in early July, which makes her a Cancer Sun), but she is not the main character. Blair was and still is, because she's a Scorpio, like me. The powers that be want us to think Serena is the main character because she's the first important face we see in the series, but instead, more depressingly, Serena is the lens through which pretty much every man on *Gossip Girl* is seen, just like the MPDGs of the era.

Serena has wild, flowing hair. She's carefree. She's fun. She's open, sexually (allegedly, because though she's slut-shamed a lot on the show, I don't think we see the evidence of her promiscuity) and intellectually. She loves to roam, she loves to explore, she loves to pull people out of their comfort zones. She's just trying to figure out this little thing called life. She threw her cell phone in a municipal trash can so she couldn't get phone calls anymore! What a wild and crazy gal! (Note: All of this is way easier and more palatable when you're an heiress.) But she also has dark secrets, and a dark past, and her mommy didn't care and her daddy didn't love her. Textbook MPDG stuff here.

We've already talked about how Lily never set Serena up for success in relationships because Lily never showed Serena and Eric examples of successful romantic relationships. She bounced from billionaire to billionaire to secure that bag, stay relevant, and keep busy enough that she never had to be alone with her own thoughts. Serena had straight-up bad parents who chased clout and money instead of actually parenting their children, so it's no wonder that Serena is pretty lost throughout the whole series. Serena attaches herself to the men on the show as a means of finding some sort of unconditional love and acceptance, because she never got anything resembling that from her mother or father. These guys were usually older, and not to say "daddy issues," but . . . daddy issues. Serena is certainly not stupid—she got into Brown as a legacy but she also went to Columbia—and she's warm and caring. She's six feet tall in good heels. She's a catch, if and when she wanted a partner to fulfill her. She just was never told she was worthy of anything, so she slipped into a trope of needing to always be positioned as an ingenue or muse for a man. Blech!

The typical MPDG character fulfills a fantasy for a male character because she sweeps into his life to save him from himself, puffing him up and sending him out into the world to conquer whatever it was he was scared of. The MPDG herself, though, never finds resolution beyond him, because who cares? She's just a girl! She's just there to fix him and skeddadle when her work is done. Time to disappear! Serena is the MPDG of *Gossip Girl* because the majority of her storylines include finding, keeping, hating, or losing a man. They want the idea of her, and never really her. We flattened the Bechdel test on this one, you guys.

Aaron Rose remembered Serena from her cute, quirky days at Camp Suisse where they talked about a caterpillar named Cedric. He was an artist, so, of course, he used Serena as his muse. But then when it turned out he was dating other people and that wasn't her thing, he was annoyed and she was no longer his muse. He didn't really care about her feelings—only about how she made him feel—and then he was out.

Tripp Vanderbilt was married, but something about Serena made him feel alive despite his boring-ass political campaign, so of course, he was smitten with her. But then he left her to die following a car accident. (Lame.)

And Dan? Where do we start with Dan Humphrey? Dan romanticized Serena so much that he started an online gossip blog to keep tabs on her—I would say that is also using her as a muse, but is it the same thing when it's so goddamn creepy? Then, when the going got tough and life got more complicated the more they got to know each other, Dan backed away, because he wanted the fun-loving, beautiful, adventurous girl he saw in the hallways and not the fully formed person she actually was, vulnerabilities and all. Yes, they shared a half-sibling and their parents wanted to date, but those are just technicalities. I have no idea how they ended up together at the end when Dan basically only used her to end his writer's block. She didn't have a say in any of it—he just wanted her to stand there and look pretty.

Only two men really respected Serena for who she was: Nate, who simply always wanted the best for her, and Carter Baizen. Honestly, she should have ended up with Carter. He knew Serena's background, he respected her, and he was happy to let her be who she was. They both had weird pasts and they both tried to be better for the other. And he looked like Sebastian Stan, which is never a problem.

Gossip Girl's 7 Most Annoying Characters

Jenny Humphrey

It pains me to write this because Jenny started out so strong, especially when she found her footing in standing up to

Taylor Momsen, who played Jenny, decided to quit acting and work with her band, The Pretty Reckless, full time. She was written off the show but appeared in the series finale.

Photo by Jeffrey Ufberg/WireImage/Getty Images.

Blair and the minions. But as soon as Taylor Momsen, who played Jenny, wanted off the show, it all went to pot. (See also Mischa Barton as Marissa Cooper in Season Three of *The O.C.*.) The bigger the eyeliner, the brattier she got, until she was literally banned from the island of Manhattan. (Which no one knew was a thing until Blair said it.)

William Van Der Woodsen

Serena's dad came into the picture much later into the series, because he was treating Lily for cancer. But he was instead giving her medicine that actually made her sick, and she didn't have cancer. It's giving Gypsy Rose. And then he pretended to love Ivy and threw her out at the end. Boy, bye.

Vanessa Abrams

I always felt like the writers didn't quite know what to do with Vanessa—she acted as a sort of lower-middle-class foil and sense of reason against the uber-wealthy characters on the show, but she mostly came off as a know-it-all who was always palling around with the 1 percent-ers she claimed to loathe.

Bart Bass

I love Robert John Burke and his body of work, but Bart Bass was one of the only characters on *Gossip Girl* who, over six seasons, never grew an inch. Even Georgina Sparks developed a moral code, even if it only made sense to her.

Agnes Andrews

Why are we setting Jenny's clothes on fire? I'm all for disrupting staid, archaic industries and ways of doing business, but damn, Jenny was your friend. Willa Holland was typecast for a long time. (See also Caitlin Cooper in *The O.C.*)

Louis Grimaldi

Louis went from prince to frog as he soured on Blair after their wedding, but the worst of it was when he paid off Chuck's therapist to leak info about Chuck so that Chuck would slowly go mad. We've seen evil on *Gossip Girl*, but it was like, fun evil. Georgina evil. Louis is just fucked up.

Sage Spence

If we wanted to see teenagers act out, we would have watched Seasons 1–5 again.

6

THE CHUCK AND BLAIR OF IT ALL

Any soap opera, teen or otherwise, has its share of maligned romantic relationships, mostly because it's necessary to keep pairing and repairing the cast of characters to keep viewers tuning in and things hot and spicy (aka that very anticlimactic threesome we just spoke about in the previous chapter). But, I'm here to burst everyone's bubble to declare that, although they're endgame, Chuck and Blair are the least shippable couple in the entire series due to their outright abusive and toxic back-and-forth relationship. Not that I'm looking to soapy teen dramas for relationships to emulate, but Chuck and Blair is not the one that young people should use as a foundation for their own.

Examinations like this are all about context, right? So bend the space–time continuum and journey back to the early aughts for a moment. The clock moved from 1999 to the year 2000 and the unimaginable Y2K hadn't happened, that is to say, the clocks didn't revert back to 0 and make us time travelers (that was what that was, right?). We were in a new millennia and it was a whole new world for the taking. Except that whole new world thing didn't really come true for women in any real sense. Feminism was maligned (oops, it still is), much of the media at the time was exceptionally fatphobic, homophobic, and misogynist. Think Renée Zellweger having to gain weight to play Bridget Jones in *Bridget Jones' Diary* and ending up looking like ::checks notes:: a normal woman, with the implication that anyone who was above a size 2 was an ogre (Anne Hathaway was also allegedly asked to gain weight for *The Devil Wears Prada* so she could be the, as they say in the movie, "smart, fat girl" as a size 6). Jessica Simpson was "fat" because she wore high-waisted jeans. Paparazzi purposefully tried to take as many "upskirt" photos of female celebrities as they could. Gossip blogger Perez Hilton slut-shamed women Britney Spears and Paris Hilton and outed as many closeted gay actors as he could. And don't forget drawing little white squiggles (use your imagination) on famous women's faces, especially their mouths! And leaking nude photos, sometimes of minors, complete with nasty nicknames! For the record, Hilton has apologized for his past actions, calling himself, "young and dumb" at the time, but, um, ok? Feels convenient to me in 2026. In the 2000s, women were supposed to have agency and have conquered whatever wave of feminism we were in at the time, but mostly it was the same hot garbage of being told you weren't thin enough or smart enough and you should be grateful for whatever scraps you got from the guys in charge. So, same as 2026.

THE CHUCK AND BLAIR OF IT ALL

So, what does this have to do with Blair Waldorf? To me, Blair Waldorf is power. She is poised and rich and classy and beautiful and intelligent and manipulative and strategic and bossy and kind and vulnerable. Chuck is sexually aggressive from the pilot, trying to coerce Serena into having sex with him because he had the chef at the Palace Hotel make her her favorite truffle grilled cheese and later attempting to rape Jenny Humphrey at the Kiss on the Lips party. Over the course of the entire series of *Gossip Girl*, Blair had a remarkable character arc, evolving from a mean queen bee high-school student to a fully formed woman with vulnerabilities and life experience, so why did she stay with Chuck all that time, especially when he lacked the same level of evolution and was distinctively awful to her throughout the series? So much more was demanded of and is still demanded of women (we're speaking in heteronormative terms here, but the point stands) that they should have to fix a broken man in order to be worthy of love. Blair can exist without Chuck, but Chuck cannot exist without Blair. Chuck is the male loneliness epidemic personified. If Blair bails on Chuck, it is because she doesn't love him enough, but if Chuck breaks up with Blair, it's because his fee-fees are hurting inside. If their entire relationship was them taking turns pushing the other away, Blair should have pushed Chuck far and run for the hills. Don't believe me? Here is a list, chronologically, of everything Blair and Chuck did to each other over the course of the series.

Chuck and Blair's dalliances start unofficially at the Kiss on the Lips party in Season 1, where they're both pissed that Serena showed her face and ruined their respective nights. One revenge plot against Serena later, things really start heating up after Blair and Nate break up, then Blair plays a burlesque dancer at Chuck's new club and Blair and Chuck spend their first night together in Chuck's limo. It's an iconic moment with an iconic bit of music supervision. Blair, unsure of her heart, bounces between Chuck and Nate for most of the season. When Blair is back with Nate, Chuck is extremely jealous and holds his and Blair's dalliance over her head. After a pregnancy scare, Chuck finds out that Blair has slept with both Chuck and Nate in a short amount of time, and Chuck tells Blair she's used up and dirty and that he could never want her again. Luckily, Georgina Sparks comes back into town and Chuck and Blair have to reunite in order to formulate a plan to take her down. In the Season 1 finale, Chuck gives an impromptu best man speech at his father's wedding to Lily, and that speech is all about how he wants to be with Blair. But the speech in itself is very indicative of Chuck's whole "won't take no for an answer" vibe, saying, "in the face of true love, you don't just give up. Even if the object of your affection is begging you to." Yes, you give up when someone tells you to go away. Nevertheless Chuck and Blair try again, which takes us to Chuck abandoning Blair before their planned summer in Europe.

THE CHUCK AND BLAIR OF IT ALL

Season 2 opens with Chuck sleeping with a bevy of women in the Hamptons and Blair with Marcus Beaton, who is a Lord. She doesn't know that in the beginning. But Marcus doesn't know that Blair doesn't love him, so they're even. Chuck investigates Marcus because he doesn't trust him, then Chuck gets erectile dysfunction because no women do it for him like Blair does. Chuck also entraps Blair into kissing him because he pretends he's Marcus, then Blair tries to get Chuck to seduce Vanessa for fun, saying that if he does it, she'll sleep with him. (Isn't that the plot of the 1999 romantic thriller *Cruel Intentions*?) Then the chase flips, with Chuck demanding Blair say "I love you," and she says she never will. Then Blair becomes obsessed with getting Chuck to have sex with her, and through some back and forth, they put their coupling on ice because they're both "not ready" for a relationship. I'll say. There are more games but I'm exhausted already, so let's fast forward to Bart Bass "dying" (he doesn't really, but play along). Chuck is understandably devastated and Blair tells Chuck she'll stand by him because she loves him and Chuck tells her not to come looking for him. Chuck loses control of his father's hotels, Chuck takes it out on Blair, and Blair says she's done. Blair doesn't get into Yale, Blair cozies up to Nate again, Chuck gets mad. Chuck has sex with Vanessa, who was dating Nate. Chuck sabotages Blair's prom experience with Nate but rigs the Prom Queen voting so Blair wins. Serena encourages Blair to tell Chuck how she feels about him, but a

Gossip Girl blast ruins all that. Then, Blair and Chuck admit they want each other and they get together for realsies.

This is just the first two seasons of Chuck and Blair. I'll speed this up for your sake. In Season 3, Chuck and Blair are together but play jealous games to keep things hot and steamy. (Aren't they like 18, btw? This is young for this, no?) Blair accuses Chuck of cheating, Chuck buys The Empire Hotel, Blair goes to NYU, they use each other back and forth some more, Blair expedites Chuck's liquor license of his new club, he gets mad, they say they should trust each other more. Chuck meets his alleged mother, Blair supports Chuck through that, Chuck's uncle Jack says he can have the hotels back for a night with Blair. At Dorota's wedding, Blair tells Chuck that she'll stay with him only because they're both sick twisted people. Then they break up. After exposing Serena's father, William, for poisoning Lily into thinking she had cancer, Chuck tells Blair he'll be at the top of the Empire State building and if she's not there by 7:01, they're donezo. She doesn't show because Dorota goes into labor. Then Chuck sleeps with Jenny, who he tried to rape in the pilot episode. Chuck gets shot while in Europe.

In Season 4, Blair says Chuck has been MIA and she just wants a date, but then she meets seemingly hot prince Louis and they get together. Chuck is in Paris with a new woman, Eva. Blair tells Chuck she doesn't want him and Chuck has Eva come back to New York. Blair is jealous and tries to blackmail Eva because Eva was a sex worker many moons ago. At his gala later that night, Blair attempts to tell him but he tells her he doesn't care. Blair breaks Eva and Chuck up and Chuck declares war. They try to ruin each other's lives for a bit, then they call a truce and sign a literal notarized peace treaty, because they are dramatic teenagers with too much money. Then, they have hate sex while declaring their hate. Then, they keep hooking up in secret but decide they can't be together until they're both successful individually. Chuck starts dating Raina Thorpe, Blair gets jealous and kisses Dan. When Chuck finds that last part out, he wants her back and Blair says her kiss with Dan made her want Chuck. They say they want a future but put it all on hold. Blair accepts Louis' proposal and Chuck gets violent, shattering a window and injuring Blair. Chuck saves Blair from dying in a fire set by Raina's dad, then they have sex. The season ends with a positive pregnancy test.

Season 5 has Blair prepping for her wedding to Louis and Chuck on a bender. Blair is pregnant with Louis' baby. Louis pays Chuck's therapist to drive him crazy. Blair is iffy about their marriage, so she's going to take her unborn baby and ride back to Chuck, who is waiting in the wings. But then they get into a bad car accident and Blair loses her baby. Chuck died, flatlining in the hospital, but he's brought back to life after Blair makes a promise to the heavens above that she'll marry Louis if Chuck lives. Chuck stalks Blair and tries to stop the wedding. They confess they love each other, which Georgina films and plays during Blair's wedding ceremony. Louis is pissed but marries her anyway. Then Blair gets together with Dan and divorces Louis. Everyone finds that Bart is alive. Blair chooses Chuck. Again.

The last season is more of the same, albeit with a pseudo-happy ending. Blair and Chuck make a pact that they can't be together until Chuck takes Bass Industries back from his father and Blair is a real-life fashion designer. They find out that Bart is breaking federal laws by selling oil in Saudi Arabia but saying it's horses (?) and Bart tells Chuck to move to Moscow. Bart tries to crash the plane but Chuck's ok, Bart takes a swing at Chuck, Bart falls off the roof. Blair is there, too. They get married so that Blair can't testify against Chuck. Bart's death is ruled an accident, and then we flash-forward five years: Chuck and Blair are still married and have a little boy named Henry. They live in a townhouse and are happily ever after.

After reading all of the trials and tribulations of Blair and Chuck over six years, let's pose a series of questions: are Blair and Chuck a stable couple? Is this a relationship you would want a son, daughter, friend, or other loved one to emulate? Do these people have way too much time on their hands? No, no, and yes. And I realize that we are talking about fictional characters here, this is media being made for young, impressionable viewers that may not have had any formative romantic relationships yet. Chuck and Blair are not an example of a good relationship, and, especially looking back on their entire arc, I would think it irresponsible to pretend they are shippable and without fault. They are endgame, so people think it's romance, but it's really just toxicity at its finest. And this sort of toxic behavior was rampant even before *Gossip Girl* hit screens. "If you think about the stuff that came before it, [it was] almost like par for the course in 1980s movies, stuff that those guys were raised on," according to journalist Jessica Pressler. "It's like all this kind of casual sexual assault that happens and that. . . . They probably dealt with it as progressively as they could have at the time."

Despite the many bad-news moments between Blair and Chuck in the series, producers on *Gossip Girl* doubled down during the show's tenure on the idea that Blair and Chuck were the fun ones. In 2017, Joshua Safran told *Vulture*, "Serena and Dan were the original couple because they're in the pilot," said Safran. "But it was always Chuck and Blair, and we always loved writing for them." In 2011, Safran told *Entertainment Weekly* that in the Season 4 episode where Chuck injures Blair, "It's very clear that Blair is not *afraid* in those moments, for herself." He goes on to explain that their relationship is volatile but it's not abuse "when it's the two of them" together. "[Chuck] punches the glass because he has rage, but he has never, and will never, hurt Blair," Safran said. "He knows it and she knows it, and I feel it's very important to know that she is *not* scared—if anything, she is scared for Chuck—and what he might do to himself, but she is never afraid of what he might do to her. Leighton and I were very clear about that." Safran also said that, at that time, Blair still believed she could have her "fairytale" with Chuck.

Sitting here fifteen years later, it feels too convenient and a cop-out to say, well, if Blair was OK with Chuck punching windows, we should all be OK with Chuck punching windows. If you see something, say something, and I'm gonna say, Blair (and any other person out there reading this that's in a similar relationship), you deserve better. Find a partner in charge of their emotions and faculties, as a baseline minimum. The bar is in hell. Telling viewers that they can have the fairytale with a partner who may not be right for them, that might be abusive, that is definitely the wrong fit, if they only just try a little harder is a damaging take. If your person is broken, you can fix them. If they're hurt, you just have to wait it out. If you reject them, well, that's on you. If they hurt you and apologize, maybe you should accept it, because if you're not scared, it doesn't count. There is no agency for them to make things better, and no need. It's all on you as a person. Also, Chuck may not have hurt Blair physically, but he did emotionally, many, many times.

It's interesting to examine fan reaction to Chuck and Blair between those who watched *Gossip Girl* live as it aired from 2007 to 2012 and those who watched it once it started streaming. (It was initially available on Netflix in 2011, and since then has bounced between Netflix and HBO Max.) Whether it's a generational difference or just an acknowledgment of the changing social mores of each respective cultural moment, the online *Gossip Girl* FanForum and commentariat of original viewers were much more likely to celebrate Blair and Chuck's relationship and push all the uncomfy assault and abuse under the rug, as Lori Bindig points out in her book *Gossip Girl: A Critical Understanding*. Per Bindig, some commenters insist that Chuck Bass is not a rapist and that any sexually aggressive acts were instead performed by "Chankie, Chuck's more evil twin who hits on [Serena] and [Jenny] in the pilot." Y'all, we are so unwilling to tell a man that he is wrong that we have to invent an evil twin to justify the behavior. What? These commenters also wildly dismiss Chuck's lack of growth over time in the series, saying that he shouldn't be judged for the assaults in the pilot, because he changed in each subsequent season. (Where? It is this author's opinion that he did not.) The *Gossip Girl* FanForum was shut down over a decade ago, but thankfully Reddit is still around. The r/GossipGirl subreddit has dozens and dozens of current threads questioning Chuck's behavior, with post titles like "unpopular opinion: you quite literally HAVE to get over Chuck in pilot to enjoy the show" and "The way Blair was treated after losing her virginity to Chuck." There are still deniers that Chuck did anything wrong, but at least there is some sort of collective consciousness that's ready to say, "Hey, this isn't right." As recently as 2024, new posts on r/GossipGirl brought up the 2017 allegations against Ed Westwick, who plays Chuck, as a lens in which to examine Chuck and Blair's relationship and the context of *Gossip Girl* itself.

In 2017, allegations surfaced that Westwick had raped two women in 2014 after separate nights of partying. A third woman claimed he groped her. Of the allegations, Westwick said on social media,

> It is disheartening and sad to me that as a result of two unverified and provably untrue social media claims, there are some in this environment who could ever conclude I have had anything to do with such vile and horrific conduct. I have absolutely not, and I am cooperating with the authorities so that they can clear my name as soon as possible.

After an investigation by the Los Angeles Police Department, Los Angeles County District Attorney's Office declined to pursue charges against Westwick due to insufficient evidence. According to documents provided to *People*, prosecutors said that even though both alleged rape victims cooperated with the police and provided access to witnesses to the alleged assaults, there was not enough information to satisfy the burden of proof for the prosecution. According to *Entertainment Weekly* in 2017, the District Attorney's Office said there were "a number of other women who accused the actor of 'unwanted touching,' but those incidents were reportedly outside of the statute of limitations for criminal proceedings."

Does Chuck love Blair, or does he simply strive to possess Blair like he does other women? A running trope in the beginning seasons of the show is that Chuck has sex with an array of women in his father's employ—an imbalance of power if I ever saw one, as I'd imagine it's hard for a cocktail waitress who depends on shift work and tips to make rent could effectively say no to the advances of the spoiled heir of a hotel magnate.

Shari Weiss, a passionate teen drama expert and writer of the TeenDramaWhore Substack, agrees, telling me that there's no way that Chuck Bass could be the romantic lead of a show in 2024. "We had no idea the way that the culture was going to change, but I think that one of the enduring problems with the show is that we had this character who, in the first episode, tries to force himself on two people," she said. "Then, a number of episodes later [he comes] into this romantic lead position with Blair, but then mistreats her horribly after they have their first time. The rest of this series is him mistreating her, abusing her emotionally, abusing her physically." In 2007, Chuck served as the sort of Upper East Side anti-hero in a TV landscape full of anti-heroes like Don Draper and Walter White, but neither of those men were teenagers and positioned to deliver a fairytale romance. They were just grown, fucked-up men, not a teenager positioning as Heathcliff. "We had that flash-forward at the very end, and Chuck and Blair have this child and, maybe miraculously, the physical and emotional abuse has ended," Weiss said. "You know, he's grown up, he's turned a corner. But [Chuck and Blair are a] really terrible example, far worse than any of the boundary-pushing sexual things that the show did, and I don't think that they've really ever answered for it."

Westwick married actor Amy Jackson in Italy in August 2024, with former *Gossip Girl* cast member Kelly Rutherford in attendance. *People* covered their nuptials in an exclusive and gushed over the proceedings, highlighting everything from the food to the flowers to the picturesque surroundings. "There's this dichotomy in the culture, I think, between who we give a pass and who we don't," Weiss said,

> And certainly if Ed Westwick got married at the time the allegations were coming out [in 2017], he was not going to get the *People* spread that he ended up getting. He was once again presented as this dashing, handsome man who got the beautiful girl. I don't know whether he did the things that he was accused of. I couldn't possibly sit here and proclaim that, but there's something uncomfortable about it all, that there were these allegations and we've just moved on.

All media is consumed through some sort of a lens. When we watch our favorite shows, we're seeing it as a part of the current zeitgeist and our own lived experience. When we watch it back, it's natural to point out plot holes or outdated technology or miscommunications that never would have happened had characters just texted or called instead of traveling all the way from Brooklyn to the Upper East Side (an hour ride on the subway, more in traffic, IYKYK) to deliver news. There are things you never noticed and things that you would no longer accept. But in the case of Chuck and Blair, their toxicity and abusive relationship wasn't OK in 2007, and it's definitely not OK today.

Chuck and Blair are the most popular "endgame" couple on *Gossip Girl*, though their relationship is largely toxic, with manipulation, lies, and emotional abuse throughout.

Photo by Brian Ach/WireImage/Getty Images.

Gossip Girl's 11 Worst Romantic Pairings

Rachel Carr and Dan

As Rufus said, there's no reason for a student to be meeting with a teacher off-campus and after-hours. Say it with me now: predator! Rachel Carr walked so Ezra Fitz from *Pretty Little Liars* could run.

Cringiest Moment: Rachel losing her first salaried job because she decided she needed to hook up with a student.

Dan and Blair

A meeting of the minds, sure, but nothing else. This one was like the writer's room said, "what if we break girl code?"

Cringiest Moment: Dan catching feelings after he and Blair kiss for the first time, and Blair being all, "yeah that guy's like my brother." Talk about a hit to the ego.

Nate and Catherine

Having a summer fling with a married woman may be very Upper East Side, and I love Madchen Amick, who played Catherine, but Nate, there are so many women your own age! How about we try that?

Cringiest Moment: Nate making Catherine jealous at the White Party with her husband inches away.

Nate and Sage

Again, Nate, what did I say about your own age? She is a teenager.

Cringiest Moment: That there was no joy, resolution, or point to this pairing. And that Sage was Jenny if Jenny was a bigger spoiled brat.

Nate and Vanessa

Alright, fine, we've hit Goldilocks levels with Vanessa being Nate's age. But now we've fallen over into "boring and have nothing in common," so this one is a big pass on my part.

Cringiest Moment: Vanessa being mad at Nate for wanting to take an internship at the mayor's office. The joke's on her here, because in the series finale, there's talk of him becoming mayor.

Jenny and Chuck

Chuck tried to sexually assault Jenny in the first season, and then she loses her virginity to him? No thanks.

Cringiest Moment: When Gossip Girl blasted the fact that she lost her virginity to Chuck. This is weird especially because *Gossip Girl was Jenny's brother.*

Rufus and Ivy

Rufus went from Lily to Ivy? At least he ended up with '90s rock icon Lisa Loeb.

Cringiest Moment: Honestly, the whole thing. This one was the stuff of nightmares. Every time they kiss on an episode, I have to look away.

Serena and Colin

What is it with this show and dating teachers? Colin was a visiting professor at Columbia but still.

Cringiest Moment: Damn, Serena—this man wanted to be with you so badly that he quit his teaching job (not that he needed it), and you broke up with him anyway? Cold as ice.

Dan and Olivia

He was a boy, she was a star, what could go wrong? Dan had already dated Serena and was kinda jealous of her socialite status, so how did he think he could be with a legitimately famous person?

Cringiest Moment: An unnecessary threesome with Vanessa.

Blair and Louis

This is what happens when you sell little girls the dream of meeting a prince and becoming a princess . . . sure, he's handsome, but he is actually a mean ole sociopath who paid off Chuck's therapist to say something that would make Chuck hurt himself.

Cringiest Moment: Louis telling Blair after their nuptials that he didn't love her but that she would have to be his wife in public and do what he says. Yikes.

Serena and Tripp

The Broadway girlie in me is always overjoyed that Aaron Tveit graced my screen on *Gossip Girl*, but Serena having an affair with Nate's married politician cousin was never going to be a good idea.

Cringiest Moment: When Tripp left Serena unconscious at the scene of a car accident and moved her dead-fish body to make it look like it was all her fault.

7

THE FASHION AND THE MUSIC

The Fashion

What good is a zeitgeist-y teen show if it doesn't have an undeniable effect on youth culture, namely in fashion and music? *Gossip Girl* costume designer Eric Daman and music supervisor Alexandra Patsavas are responsible for everything from bringing the headband and colored tights back into popular dressing culture to launching the careers of ultra-famous bands, and it's all because they were picked to work on a little teen drama called *Gossip Girl*.

I was studying abroad in London in 2007 when *Gossip Girl* premiered in the United States. I already loved fashion, but I was thrown into a whole new world of possibilities between being in Europe and watching the show. Being a tall blonde who did not like to blow dry her hair automatically made me a Serena, and I can tell you I bought roughly six pairs of faux suede knee-high boots at the Primark on Oxford Street (yes, they all fell apart instantly, and I was 19 and the exchange rate was 2 dollars to 1 pound, and god, everything was expensive). A vest? Loved it! A big statement necklace? In! Totally in! And all around me, I watched other girls and women channel Blair in colorful tights and wide, prim headbands. Something was going on.

That something was costume designer Eric Daman, the genius mind behind the clothes of all of your favorite shows, including *Sex and the City* and *Gossip Girl*. Journalist Tyler McCall told me:

> Eric Damon is a genius and he's so brilliant at what he does. I think that the costumes just so immediately tell a story about who the characters are, whether it's Blair's kind of Type-A control freak, like everything matches and like the headband is a finishing touch, and then it's like Serena. Free spirited. Very like Kate Moss, Coachella vibes kind of situation going on.
>
> You know, Jenny's whole trajectory, I think, is told really well through fashion from being this kind of naive little girl into being a little Blair into becoming kind of herself in this little fashion school rebel. I mean, even the guys . . . a lot of times, I think men don't get as much storytelling through costume. I mean I think menswear in general is just harder, but Chuck's kind of dapper, new dandy vibe tells something different about him than Nate.

"When I first got the script for the *Gossip Girl* pilot, I wasn't familiar with the book series, and I was like, 'Oh, a pilot for a TV series; it's just not for me.' There was a moment where I

THE FASHION AND THE MUSIC

wasn't even gonna read the script, and then my boyfriend was like, 'Why don't you just read the first page?'" Daman told *Fashionista*. "I read the first page, and it totally dragged me right in; my teen mean girl came out immediately, and I was just obsessed. Then I read the book series, and I just felt in me that I had to be a part of this project—and I'm very happy that I did."

Daman initially got the job through a connection with *Gossip Girl* producer Amy Kaufman, who introduced him to [co-creator] Stephanie Savage. They hit it off immediately. In a *Gossip Girl* DVD featurette, Savage recounted their first meeting: "The first time that I met Eric . . . I had come with my binder and he had come with his binder . . . and as I was talking about Sienna Miller and bohemian chic and Kate Moss, Eric was pulling out his [ideas] that were matching my [ideas]," Savage said.

"I'd say 75 percent to 85 percent of the tear sheets were the exact same in each book, Damon said. "It was really quite thrilling . . . oh, we can actually maybe get to do something very New York and kind of fashion forward . . . what we could do with the costumes and who these girls were going to be and who these boys were and like what kind of world this is set in."

Once Daman reviewed the books and got a very real sense of who each character was and how he would dress them, it was totally on. "It was character driven from the get-go, especially with Blair and Leighton [Meester]. Who Leighton is in real life and how she dresses on the red carpet is so different from Blair," Daman told *Teen Vogue*. "Leighton's a bit more avant-garde in her fashion choices than Blair would be. Serena and Blake became a bit more symbiotic. I feel like Serena's style definitely drifted into Blake's real life, and as Blake became the fashion icon that she is, also kind of floated into Serena's life. They co-inspired each other."

Meester confirms that Daman's costuming made it easier for her to channel Blair's Upper East Side Attitude. "I'll be blocking and rehearsing the scene, and I'm like, 'Okay this will go really well,' and then I put on the clothes and then suddenly I'm the character," she said in the featurette. "[Blair] has a very high-end sense of style. Everything she wears is pretty much designer. She loves high-waisted skirts, she loves crisp jackets . . . the best way to describe it is that she's appropriate. If she's going to sushi dinner, she dresses exactly like you're supposed to. If she's going to a wedding, that's exactly how she dresses. . . . It just always makes sense."

No one can mention Blair Waldorf without making reference to her oft-talked-about accessory. "Blair has her signature headband . . . we imagine it sort of as like her crown. It's her little tiara that she puts on every morning, like 'I am the queen, therefore I must mark my queenness with my little headband.' Her followers also don their headbands as a way to show allegiance to her," Savage said.

Blake Lively's Serena was inspired by a heavy dose of boho chic, but a great deal of thought went into helping Lively look that effortless on TV. "Serena kind of just picks up whatever she finds on the floor and kind of has a tousled, sexy, just-got-out-of-bed look . . . very natural just very thrown together," Daman said.

> It sounds really easy, but when you're trying to put the outfits together to make it look like it's just thrown together, it is really a very difficult challenge. Blake already had that kind of thing to her, you know, she just was like very relaxed and very natural and just had a kind of this innate sensibility to her that really lent itself to becoming Serena.

"Serena has all these beautiful designer clothes but she would wear them with her old jeans and her great boots and her slouchy cap and look amazing," said Savage. Soon, Lively and Daman were working together to help come up with her signature Serena look. "Blake wanted to play with the clothes and be a part of it, and I think Blake and Serena had a symbiotic relationship, in a way, stylistically," Daman told *Fashionista*. "I'd bring in all these racks of things that I thought were perfect for Serena and outfits that had some architectural design—like if we need a party look or a school look—and have that laid out to work with her on."

> But then we had a wonderful back and forth of what each outfit was going to be and how it went together. She got more and more involved in that way as Serena grew and as Blake grew. When she first came in, I think she was open to deferring to me

because she was just learning. She was wide-eyed; she loved it all so much and wanted to be around the fashion and wanted to learn about it all.

Kelly Rutherford, who played Lily, also collaborated with Daman quite a bit on her looks. "Eric . . . was a dream to work with. There were so many characters and [all of us actors] had our own ideas and visions," Rutherford told *Fashionista*. "He was so patient and kind and would just bring the most incredible clothes to choose from. Even if I or somebody else requested a specific brand, he would always find it and bring it in. It was very collaborative."

Rutherford was basically channeling Lily directly with the help of one of her own special collections. "Things we couldn't get from elsewhere, like the Hermes bags, I would bring from home just to help the character. Lily Van der Woodsen was a character I could really explore fashion with," she told *Luminaire*.

Gossip Girl also tackled menswear, which, in my opinion, gets forgotten about but can be just as impactful in developing a character if it's done correctly. "There really is a guy in New York who's wearing a carnation in his lapel. He would wear a bowler hat. He would wear a white suit or a red suit or pay a lot of attention to what kind of shoes," Savage said in the DVD featurette. "Chuck's clothes are at times eccentric, at times classic . . . he's not scared of a bit of color. It's never bland but it's totally reflective of his personality," Ed Westwick, who played Chuck, added.

"[Chuck], he was kind of our editorial answer to the male Upper East Side boy . . . a little bit of an urban edge, you know, keeping track with lots of really great cutting edge sneakers . . . like the brand new Nikes that just got shipped from Japan that only he has a pair of," Daman said in the DVD featurette. "And of course his signature scarf which has become its own kind of entity. We got the scarf approved, we got the scarf on TV, and all of a sudden someone leaked [it] and the stores sold out of them in a week."

Of course, a show about Upper East Side private school teens meant spending some time with Upper East Side private school teens to see what they were wearing, doing, and spending their money on.

"I actually went and hung out around the Upper East Side [private] schools like Chapin. I wanted to do real research because I'm an East Village kid and I'm a part of fashion, but that world is a very different world and I wanted to go see it for myself—and this is before iPhones," Daman told *Fashionista*.

> It was incredible to see, these girls were all running in posses that were designer brand influenced. All the girls wearing Tory Burch flats—this was when Tory Burch flats were a big thing—were hanging out together. Then there was a group of girls carrying Marc Jacobs bags or girls carrying Coach. It felt like there was a brand identity and how they were styling themselves had to do with that brand.

Now came the hard part of figuring out how to make the school uniform interesting, since the school uniform is most of the outfitting for the first few seasons. Daman told *Fashionista*:

> Serena comes back from having left the school, and she wears her school's uniform skirt from her freshman year, so it's a different plaid than the other girls are wearing. She's a rule-breaker, so maybe she just wears T-shirts and is a little bit less formal about it, but as long as it was a white shirt of some sort, we could get away with it.
>
> I think it worked really, really well that she didn't wear collared shirts, and that we saved that for Blair and her cronies. That was the initial thing that set the two looks apart, that we took a little bit of liberty; Serena was such a free spirit that she was like, "I'm just going to wear my henley and my skinny tie," and Blair's in a ruffled blouse and a cape. It just really differentiates who they are.

Although viewers instantly knew that what Blair and Serena wore was cool (and since it was mostly young women watching the show, the attempt to emulate it was instantaneous), the network . . . didn't necessarily get what Daman was trying to do at first.

"For Season One of the show, my job just became protecting Eric [Daman] so that he could do what he wanted to do, and a lot of the ideas that he were pitching were not mainstream ideas, like Serena has a look in the pilot where she's wearing shorts with tights, and I got so much pushback," Savage told Jessica Szohr on her podcast. "Every time that happened, I would just write an essay about why shorts were the new mini skirt."

Daman was frustrated by the pushback, but he understood that for people who are not creatives or visionaries (and people who have to be selling advertising spots for TV), breaking new ground or trying new things can be a little nerve wracking, but it's necessary to move forward.

"It was very clear from the beginning that we wanted to editorialize television and give it this high-fashion, international flair," Daman told *Vanity Fair*. Savage added, "We talked about how the show, on the one hand, is telling this fictional story about these characters, but it's also kind of working as a lifestyle magazine."

Dressing an entire cast in dozens of costumes with dozens of wardrobe changes and hundreds of fittings is no easy endeavor, but the clothing instantly made an impact in viewers' buying patterns. "We're very lucky to have [Eric Daman] . . . he already before the show was very ahead of the trends, and now he's able to set them even more firmly," Penn Badgley, who played Dan, said in the featurette. "I'll give you a specific instance. There's a boot Blake wore in an episode. It's like these knee-high sort of suede . . . it's like a $50 boot, which relatively speaking on the show, it's a cheap item. And the next day, I think across the country in every store they were sold out."

Every time an episode of *Gossip Girl* aired, it would translate into sales. "During the second season, there was a front-page article in *The New York Times* about *Gossip Girl*'s fashion and how stores like Bloomingdale's couldn't keep the show's clothes on shelves," former president of the CW Dawn Ostroff told *The Hollywood Reporter*. "People watch the show the way they read a magazine: They want to know where to get the clothes, where to get the music and where to go in New York."

"You can't say that about very many shows, that what they're wearing on the show is influencing what we're seeing on the runways, but I think the *Gossip Girl* has that effect to some degree, which says a whole lot about Eric Daman and the styling and the cast who wear their clothes really, really well," then *New York Magazine* editor Amy O'Dell said in the featurette.

In an interview with *The Selfish Gift*, Savage lamented that they couldn't make a direct-to-consumer *Gossip Girl* fashion line to capitalize on the show's buzz. "[Daman] didn't make the clothes for the show—he bought the clothes and curated them and put them on the actors, but then those clothes would explode," she said.

> Iconic elements from the show would then show up in Zara and H&M or . . . I would have loved to have done more with it. . . . That was a frustrating aspect of it for me, because Warner Brothers, who made the show, the way they were set up, they were like, we don't have the apparatus to make a *Gossip Girl* clothing line. . . . In

2009, people were like, "What are you talking about? People don't watch TV to buy clothes."

Warner Brothers, she continues, was better set up to create merch for its biggest franchises, like DC Comics and Harry Potter—they couldn't set aside time and money to create an actual clothing line. The closest the show got was a *Gossip Girl*-inspired Target collection for Anna Sui and a line Eric Daman did for Kohl's, and I'm sure very many *Gossip Girl* fans are lamenting that they missed the chance to own an actual piece of the show.

They settled for "inspired by," at least, and headbands and colored tights took off like a rocket ship, mostly because these less-expensive accessories were a great way for the "everyday" girl to mimic the Upper East Side aesthetic they craved from watching *Gossip Girl* every week. Designer Nanette Lepore's clothing was featured all the time on *Gossip Girl*, and she told *Fashionista* she credits the show with boosting her bottom line even further:

"The boom of my company was so tied into that moment in time, and *Gossip Girl* I'm sure pushed that up a lot. It was better than being on the pages of a magazine. It was doing for my business what editorial would have done ten years earlier," she said. "What I think it did for people was make them feel more free about their own styling and make young girls more excited to experiment with fashion, and it was a moment in American fashion where we were just coming into our own. I think that all these things came together to really push American fashion into a boom."

And we're talking serious money here. "We probably have 50 percent more of our traffic, close to one million viewers each month, going into *Gossip Girl* than into any other show," said Travis Schneider, the founder of StarBrand Media, a company that handled e-commerce connections for shows like *Gossip Girl* and *America's Next Top Model,* told *The New York Times*. Stephanie Solomon, the fashion director for Bloomingdale's, added that *Gossip Girl* had a "profound" effect on the retail landscape as it aired.

It was an uphill climb to get there. "Fashion designers and the PR houses just really didn't want anything to do with television. There was such a stigma about the look of TV," Daman told *Fashionista*. "It's funny with PR fashion houses. They would always be like, 'Well, who else said yes? Has Chanel said yes?' Once Chanel said 'yes,' it was the deluge because Chanel really never did before. It really helped the creativity and editorialization of the look of the show—and television in general."

Of course, once the train started rolling, it was impossible to stop, with the world's biggest brands knocking, including Karl Lagerfeld from Chanel using Lively as his own muse, and *Gossip Girl* getting its very own limited-edition fashion collection, sold at Kitson, Neimann Marcus, and Saks. Daman told *Vanity Fair,*

"When we came back with Season 2, so many designers were lining up and wanting to be a part of it—they wanted their stuff on either Blake or Leighton."

It all soon became a self-fulfilling sort of prophecy, with viewers tuning in to see what the characters would wear and then shopping what the characters would wear to emulate the characters that they would tune in for . . . you get the idea. And although the show was always supposed to be fashion-forward, none of the producers of *Gossip Girl* or Daman himself could have seen this coming.

"There are looks you see on the show that you then see out in the world, and you're never quite sure, you know, was the show prescient and they knew it was coming? Or did the show create it," producer Josh Safran said in the featurette.

"It's been a great adventure to kind of see how the fashion has grown and how much we have explored and kind of started setting trends in our own way," Daman added.

"Fashion has played a really big role in the long-term success of the show. It started really in the notion of character and figuring out how we could use clothing to express who these people were," Savage continued. "It's really hard to imagine who Blair Waldorf is without thinking about her headbands or her shoe collection or her sort of Audrey Hepburn-inspired vintage outfits, or Serena without thinking of her kind of boho chic sexy dresses and her great accessories."

The Music

Equally as important as the fashion of *Gossip Girl*, in my mind, was the music. Alexandra Patsavas, the musical director on *Gossip Girl*, soundtracked basically every bit of formative millennial culture, from *Grey's Anatomy* and *The O.C.* to *Twilight* and *Gossip Girl*. There are whole bands and musical movements that we know of because Patsavas had the wherewithal and taste to say, "this would be the perfect song for this perfect scripted moment."

"[Music] is something that the executive producers, Josh [Schwartz] and Stephanie [Savage], and I talked about a great deal, actually. It's really an amalgam of indie, pop, and New York–based bands," Patsavas told *Vanity Fair*. "The music I send down to the show includes a lot of Top 40 as well as some unsigned bands from the city. So it's definitely a wide spectrum, and I think it's really that musical soup that gives the show its style."

It's helpful that Schwartz and Savage love music and have heavy opinions on it, too. If you watched their first show, *The O.C.*, you know that they launched the widespread careers of bands like The Killers, Modest Mouse, and, of course, Death Cab for Cutie (we cannot forget about Death Cab). "Josh is definitely like a big music head," Savage told Szohr on her podcast. "I loved music growing up, but I had kind of given up on music. . . . And then when we did *The O.C.*, Josh and Alex Patsavas, our music supervisor, really kind of like brought me back to life of liking indie music and recognizing that that stuff was out there. You just had to dig a little."

> We talked a lot about pop music and pop music was having a great moment when we were doing the pilot, and that stuff that we wouldn't have played on *The O.C.* . . . worked for *Gossip Girl* because there's something about New York that just leans into that sort of pop music. Just super what's coming out of people's car windows, what you're walking into a club, what you're hearing like, it's just such a melting pot of so many different sounds.

With so much music being created by talented people around the world, the way Patsavas gets them to our ears varies from moment to moment. "I send down a compilation every week or two that includes music that I think would be a good fit for the show. Music gets pitched for scripts sometimes. If there's an on-camera band, like the Pierces . . . that's something that's talked about way in advance," she told *Vanity Fair*. "The band has to be decided on and booked, and we have to make sure the songs are clearable. So sometimes the process happens way before an edited cut, and sometimes you really have to wait before you see what is on screen before pitching songs."

"I think that really we get exposed to so much music. Really excellent stuff is very self-evident. It really is, especially when you listen to so much . . . great bands really stick out," Patsavas told *VICE*.

The music on the show set the scene for the audience, but it also helped the writers' room encapsulate the feelings they wanted to put forth over the airwaves. "I loved the music on the show, I thought . . . again, that's where Stephanie did such a great job of, you know, of, of setting the tone. I have really strong musical connections to the show that aren't even in the show I write," writer Amanda Lasher told me. "I remember her referring to this once as a musical envelope, and I wrote so many episodes listening just to Tegan and Sarah . . . I would like to put together playlists and stuff that felt like it got me into that mode."

Schwartz joked that a lot of that music came at a great cost (though it was worth it!). "When you watch the pilot, there's so much music in the pilot. It's . . . it was like the record for most amount of money that they had ever spent on music, and they just wanted it to be this," he told Szohr. "It was more even than we were comfortable [spending] at times, but it was just like all these . . . it's pretty wall to wall and it all worked, but it was very expensive and we're like, 'How are you guys going to pay for all of this music?' [The network was] willing to step in and spend the money."

Damn am I glad that they spent the money, because the best moments of the show just wouldn't be the same had they chosen other music to go along with them. Chuck and Blair in the limo listening to another song wouldn't be Chuck and Blair in the limo.

THE FASHION AND THE MUSIC

Actresses Leighton Meester and Blake Lively on set. Their undone, personalized school uniforms were imitated by teens around the world.

Photo by James Devaney/WireImage/Getty Images.

Gossip Girl's 11 Best Music Moments

"The Ice Is Getting Thinner" by Death Cab for Cutie

The Episode: Season 1, Episode 18 "Much 'I Do' About Nothing"

The Moment: Schwartz and Savage's *The O.C.* was responsible for popularizing Death Cab for Cutie, but *Gossip Girl* perfected it with this moment, which showed Chuck and Blair beginning their relationship in earnest and Dan and Serena ending theirs.

"With Me" by Sum 41

The Episode: Season 1, Episode 7 "Victor, Vitrola"

The Moment: Blair and Chuck. In the limo. Real ones know nothing got better than this—the passion. The potential. The jawlines!

"Young Folks" by Peter Bjorn and John

The Episode: Season 1, Episode 1 "Pilot"

The Moment: The moment the whistling started in the opening of the pilot, you just knew there was something special about to happen.

"Tell Me A Lie" by Fratellis

The Episode: Season 2, Episode 1 "Summer, Kind of Wonderful"

The Moment: Serena and Dan are broken up, but they've taken their exceptional sexual chemistry to the Hampton Jitney, where Serena eats strawberries, falls on Dan's lap, and then drags him into the bathroom. I was going to deduct points here because clearly the writers have never experienced the smell or size of a bathroom on a bus like the Jitney, but I let this one slide.

"Wild Wolves" by Athlete

The Episode: Season 3, Episode 13 "The Hurt Locket"

The Moment: For all the problems I have with Blair and Chuck, they have the most satisfactory-soundtracked moments on the show. This one in Season 3 also features Chuck's maybe mom and her famous locket.

"Sour Cherry" by The Kills

The Episode: Season 1, Episode 14 "The Blair Bitch Project"

The Moment: This one's a favorite for a few reasons, but namely because it really sums up the attitude of the show—if you were alive and watching for the first time back in

2007, you'll remember this tough Brit-alt-rock was everywhere, and this is just a great scene watching Jenny hand what Blair gives out back to her.

"Signs" by Bloc Party

The Episode: Season 2, Episode 13 "O Brother, Where Bart Thou?"

The Moment: Eleanor and Cyrus's wedding? Not enough!

"Starpower" by Sonic Youth

The Episode: Season 3, Episode 5 "Rufus Getting Married"

The Moment: I know that Lady Gaga and No Doubt also appeared on *Gossip Girl*, but getting arguably one of the greatest American rock bands of the last fifty years to appear on a soapy teen drama was a real win for the music supervising staff.

"Believe" by The Bravery

The Episode: Season 1, Episode 2 "The Wild Brunch"

The Moment: An ideal song for Serena to walk down a New York City street and throw her flip phone in a municipal trash can.

"Whatcha Say" by Jason Derulo

The Episode: Season 3, Episode 11 "The Treasure of Serena Madre"

The Moment: Iconic for multiple reasons, firstly because the Imogen Heap sample in this song was a cultural phenomenon when it appeared on *The O.C.* a few years prior. Then *Gossip Girl* found the updated song and used it to soundtrack a *very* intense Thanksgiving dinner! Brava!

"Dark on Fire" by Turin Brakes

The Episode: Season 2, Episode 8 "Pret-a-Poor-J"

The Moment: Chuck and Blair aren't the only ones who can have their romance via music—this moment between Jenny and Nate reminds me of a time before Jenny became absolutely too annoying to function.

8

THE END, THE REBOOT, AND BEYOND

Now we have to talk about something really upsetting—the end of *Gossip Girl*. By 2012, the world was a different place. The glitz and glam of 2007 had been replaced by a recession, and being *that rich* and flaunting it wasn't cool when people were literally losing their homes and jobs. Plus, by Season 6, *Gossip Girl* had jumped the shark. Go back to the chapter you just read about Chuck and Blair, take in all of the bonkers storylines that *were just for those characters*, and extrapolate that to the entire cast. Way back then, before streamers really took over, network TV was a whopping 20–24 episodes a season, which meant a lot of air time to fill, a lot of plots to keep straight, and a lot of continuity that could be damned. It's no wonder, really, that *Gossip Girl* ran out of runway. Over six seasons, viewers saw fake cancer, a character stage his own death and then die again for realsies, a love child, every combination of hookup possible within the cast (including Rufus and a woman who could be his daughter), multiple fake identities, and enough bandage dresses to keep Hervé Léger in business until the year 3000. It's always good to know when to leave a party. *Gossip Girl* was canceled by The CW at the end of Season 5, and the producers fought for ten episodes of Season 6 to wrap things up. And on December 17, 2012, 1.5 million people watched and said goodbye.

The series finale, entitled, "New York, I Love You, XOXO," wrapped every little storyline up with a bow, even if sloppily. Bart falls off a roof to his death and Blair and Chuck get married in Central Park so they can't testify against each other with regard to Bart's suspicious demise. William comes back to the city with Lily because Bart is dead, and he drops Ivy like a bad habit. Nate, now running the *New York Spectator* because Bart is dead, is trying to find out who Gossip Girl is (Sage, too, but we don't talk about Sage) and running through a long list of people it isn't. Serena stops a plane to Los Angeles and stays in New York. Dan explains to Serena the when, how, and why he became Gossip Girl. He then gives the Gossip Girl scoop to Nate to publish in the *Spectator*. Dan is now free and unburdened. When the news is published, everyone from Mayor Mike Bloomberg to actress Rachel Bilson have opinions. (Bloomberg thought it was Dorota. Billionaires have *Gossip Girl* opinions, too, I guess.)

No one's *really* that mad about Dan being Gossip Girl minus Rufus, but Rufus lost all his credibility when he dated a 22-year-old, so, whatever, Rufus. Nate's all, "we succeeded in spite of Gossip Girl, so who cares," because he is a white man who comes from generations and generations from inherited wealth. Of course he succeeded. The only thing that ever happened to him is that his father loved snow. Blair declares Gossip Girl dead. Five years later in a flashforward in 2017, Blair and Chuck have a son, Henry, and Blair is the CEO of Waldorf Designs. Jenny has a fashion collaboration with them. Nate might run for mayor, and his paper is doing well. Lily is with William. Rufus is with 1990s rock queen Lisa Loeb. Georgina is with Jack Bass. Dan and Serena get married. And, at the very end, a Gossip Girl voiceover declares that she's really not dead, because there will always be an outsider trying to get in. You know you love her, XOXO, etc. etc.

The thing that always struck me about Dan being Gossip Girl is the amount of belief we were supposed to suspend to be OK with it and the fact that Dan must be a literal sociopath, given the amount of subterfuge and betrayal he performed reporting on the people who loved him the most. I guess Dan letting out all of Chuck Bass' secrets is one thing, since they were very much enemies for most of the show's six seasons. But Jenny? His sister? Or Serena, the girl he started the whole thing for? His *eventual wife?* If someone did this to me, I would get a restraining order, not marry them. Actually, it would be worse than a restraining order, but I shouldn't put it in print. Just in case. As far as all the other nicely tied-up stories in the finale go, I mean, fine? They were just fine. I think TV writers are damned if they do and damned if they don't when it comes to series finales. If you write what the fans want, it can end up as crowdsourced slop. If you don't, the audiences that gave you the ratings to continue and gave you a job will complain about it for years. (It's me. I am that audience.) I recognize that for as much as the writing of the show was good and it was entertaining, it was not *Mad Men*, not *Breaking Bad*, not *The Americans*. Not a writer-driven prestige drama, a show in which people would have been comfortable with a vague "Did Tony Soprano die or not," Journey-soundtracked series finale. It had to be neat and tidy, and I'm fine with Henry Bass wearing a little bowtie, because kids in bowties are always adorable. But just . . . did Gossip Girl have to be Dan?

"*Gossip Girl* is regularly in lists of the worst TV finale of all time, and I don't think that's done sensationally," TeenDramaWhore Substack creator and writer Shari Weiss said.

> I think it's because they gave an answer that didn't make sense. I remember there was this Tumblr page that was just regularly updating with all the reasons why [Dan being Gossip Girl] made no sense, and their list was bang-on . . . It's really frustrating to have this thread from the very beginning of the show and not have it pay off in a good way. There were going to be flaws no matter who they chose at this point, but it's really unfortunate the way that ended up.

That Tumblr page still exists, by the way, and it's worth a read. It's literally called "Why Dan Humphrey Can't Be Gossip

Girl," and it's perhaps an even more enduring example of why *Gossip Girl* matters—if something has no haters, it's not worth watching.

The cast and crew of *Gossip Girl* have differing opinions of Dan as creep extraordinaire and how he got there. Following the finale, executive producer and creator Stephanie Savage told *TVLine* that there was never "another choice in [their] mind" if Dan was going to be Gossip Girl. "It was always just a question of were we going to reveal it or not to reveal it. It was unclear if knowing Gossip Girl's identity was something fans would want," she said. "Maybe it was more fun for everyone to not know who Gossip Girl was and be able to speculate and come up with your own ideas." And when pressed if fans should go back and see all the inconsistencies in this change to the lore, Savage said,

> We didn't want to lean in too heavily to that idea. It was nothing that we talked to the actors about. It was nothing that we wanted to be part of Penn Badgley's performance as Dan. Or something that we wanted viewers to be actively thinking about. We were hoping to have a nice long run and we didn't want people to be preoccupied by the question of, "Who is Gossip Girl?" So we held reins loosely and didn't want to draw attention to the fact that one of our main characters might actually be Gossip Girl.

Savage's co-creator and *Gossip Girl* executive producer Josh Schwartz also maintained that Dan was Gossip Girl from day one, telling *E! News*,

We never really entertained any other ideas of who Gossip Girl was. It was whether we were going to reveal it. Interestingly, in the pilot episode, the test audience thought that Dan was Gossip Girl. We actually had to re-edit one of our sequences. It's when he's on the computer looking at Gossip Girl, the way it was edited that he was typing as the voice was coming up, people thought that they were being told that he was Gossip Girl. So we actually had to re-edit that sequence.

In 2017, executive producer Josh Safran told *Vulture*, "I always thought [Gossip Girl] was Eric until the end of season two, and I even guided it that way, but when the *New York Post* revealed it was Eric—and I still don't know how that happened, I think they were just guessing—and we realized we couldn't go down that road anymore, so we abandoned him." In 2019, Safran appeared on a panel at Vulture Festival, saying, "I like to joke that Dan was Gossip Girl because I had left the show by then. Dan was not my intended Gossip Girl, so honestly you'd have to ask someone else."

"We discussed it so much over the years and a case could be made for and against everyone," executive producer and writer Amanda Lasher said.

I don't look at it and think like, "Oh, no, it shouldn't have been Dan." But there's nobody that I feel very strongly that it should have been. . . . I remember at a certain point, we thought about revealing

THE END, THE REBOOT, AND BEYOND

Gossip Girl early. And I felt very strongly that we shouldn't, but I don't even remember how serious those things were.

Honestly, this all feels like revisionist history, considering how annoyed people are about the ending. We're seriously supposed to believe that the show's creators were dead-set on the weirdest option possible? I don't buy it. There's an old adage: If you hear hoofbeats, you should think horses, not zebras. Dan does not make sense as Gossip Girl. Period. Schwartz and Savage are not the first showrunners to insist they were always going to zig when we know they zagged—remember when Damon Lindelof and Carlton Cuse insisted that the gang on *LOST* were not in purgatory and then they all met up in a church that sure as hell seemed a lot like purgatory in the finale?—and they will not be the last. But considering that multiple other executive producers on *Gossip Girl* have hesitated to claim it was always going to be Dan, the alarms are going off, people.

"We didn't know. I mean, that finale script, when I, when I got the first version of it, we were already shooting. I mean, it was literally almost all blacked out, so we were getting the scenes like as you were showing up on set to shoot them," Zuzanna Szadkowski, who played Dorota, said.

> I think even Penn [Badgley, who played Dan] probably didn't find out until close to filming those scenes. I feel like I think a lot of people did, that it should have been Dorota, but I'm glad it wasn't.

I feel like there's a real, pure love between Dorota and Blair. . . . If Dorota has any purpose, it's there really be that like, sort of, caretaking, a warm place for Blair to fall and without those people in the story, it can be untethered. And so I think that relationship to me was very precious. . . . That would mean that there had been so much betrayal of Blair along the way.

Whether you wanted Dan to be Gossip Girl or not (it is apparent that I did not), the very fact that fans are thinking about it over fifteen years later means that *Gossip Girl* has left an indelible mark on television and culture. Every *Gossip Girl* retrospective published in the years after the show's finale laid a question of who would consider returning for a reboot or movie or afternoon special, and the results were usually mixed. In 2017, Wallace Shawn, who played Cyrus, told *Vanity Fair* he would "Jump at it." Lily Van Der Woodsen herself, Kelly Rutherford, said, "I would be completely on board. And I think they should do it soon." Leighton Meester demurred, saying that she never said never, and Blake Lively said the same to *Variety*, which I think is a nice, media-trained way of saying, "There's no way I want to go back to that, but I can't say that in an interview that will be published on the internet." And I can't argue with that—these actors aren't teenagers anymore. They have families and lives and want to do their careers as grown adults. Who wants to go back to high school? Not me.

THE END, THE REBOOT, AND BEYOND

Back to the steps of the Met: Evan Mock, Emily Alyn Lind, Thomas Doherty, Eli Brown, Jordan Alexander, Zion Moreno, and Savannah Lee Smith starred in the *Gossip Girl* reboot, which lasted two seasons on HBO Max.

Photo by Jose Perez/Bauer-Griffin/GC Images/Getty Images.

Gossip Girl fans went eight years streaming and re-streaming their favorite episodes until 2019, when original *Gossip Girl* producer Safran announced that the show was up for a reboot, this time on HBO Max, and with all new characters. At the time, Safran told *Entertainment Tonight*,

> I think it very much represents where we will be at in 2020 when the show airs. It really looks at how social media has changed. You know, the first time around, when the show started people were, like, checking in places on Foursquare and updating their locations

on Facebook. Things we would never do now because we don't want anyone to know where we are. That change alone changes the dynamic of what Gossip Girl means and how Gossip Girl interacts with the kids this day and age, so I think it's gonna be really interesting to see. The modern age reflected through Gossip Girl.

This little, minor thing called a global pandemic put the show on pause for a bit, and it debuted in July 2021 to . . . middling reviews? I'm gonna be honest here and say I watched the first season and never finished the second. I was happy with the show's casting adjustments, including more people of color and LGBTQ+ characters, since these people all exist in New York City, but for me, the *Gossip Girl* reboot just . . . fell flat, and here are some reasons why. And be warned—spoilers ahead.

1. **It lacked the simultaneous lunacy and gravitas of the original.** Having to fill airtime for 22 episodes a season meant some of the storylines in the original show were duds, but it also gave plenty of room for character development. The reboot, with much shorter seasons, couldn't have either because there wasn't room. Not every song has to be a hit, you know?
2. **There was no nostalgia.** Millennials love thinking back on the good old days, and while I understand the concerted effort to not make this Blair and Chuck Part 2, more callbacks (and not just Georgina's son) would have been nice.

I'm not saying that *Gilmore Girls* or *Sex and the City* did their reboots especially well, but they delivered more of what their nostalgia-driver viewers were seeking. *Gossip Girl 2: Electric Boogaloo* followed more of what *90210* did with their reboot, which fell flat for the same reason: too much new.

3. **There was no camp.** I was always struck by how visually bleak and dark the reboot was. Yes, we were in a post-Obama, post-Covid era, but the cinematography made the new *Gossip Girl* look like a Christopher Nolan movie. The original had colorful, over-the-top outfits, stories, music . . . and the reboot was so slick, so shiny, so dark, so blah. It wasn't *Euphoria* or *Skins* but it wasn't bright, either. It was in a sad middle ground.

4. **How Gen Z interacts with social media is boring to watch on TV.** Millennials were the last generation to straddle the digital and analog worlds, so the original *Gossip Girl* had them doing a lot of running around through New York every time *Gossip Girl* made a blast. In reality, Gen Z (and Gen Alpha, too) does a lot of interaction through text, FaceTime, private Snapchats, and the like. But does anyone want to watch that? Who wants to watch one hundred takes of a TikTok dance? One thousand navel-gazing video stitches? Drama needs face-to-face contact and the communication today is just different. (For the record, this is also why the *Pretty Little Liars* reboot didn't work today, either.)

5. **Old money vs. new money.** Generations of wealth will always be fascinating to Americans, because unless you were born into it, you're never invited into the club. You could work from rags to riches and be a self-made billionaire, and you're still never really going to belong. In old *Gossip Girl*, these were established, very wealthy families in the social register. Ultra mysterious. The new *Gossip Girl* was more new money, which we all have a better shot at than changing the circumstances of our birth. Aspirational, maybe, but more pedestrian at the same time. There is also a greater class consciousness in today's world, so perhaps folks just aren't watching super-rich people be really bad when they can turn the news on and see the exact same thing.

6. **The clothes just weren't as good.** Costume designer Eric Daman came back for the reboot, but the fashion choices weren't as iconic or trendsetting like they were the first time around. Perhaps just a saturation of the market? For the original, viewers were focused on the clothing of one show at a time. For the reboot, the fashion-obsessed are more likely to scroll Instagram than watch TV for their clothing inspo—they are getting OOTD ideas from their favorite influencers and not their favorite television shows. Also, the aforementioned class consciousness: none of the clothes are inexpensive or affordable. Which, yeah, they are rich kids, so it makes sense why Damon chose what he chose, but it's maybe slightly tone-deaf when the kids can't get jobs.

7. **The whole plot depended on a huge violation.** In the reboot, Gossip Girl was an adult. Teacher Kate Keller, played by Tavi Gevinson, restarted "Gossip Girl" the blog so that her bratty students would stop and reflect on their actions and scare themselves straight. Except that didn't work, because the youths of the show just start weaponizing all their respective secrets against each other by way of Gossip Girl. And why would it work? These kids have no frontal lobes yet. One of Kate's first "victims" is Zoya, who is new and on scholarship at Constance Billard. That will teach them! Target the poor kid! This is not to say that the original *Gossip Girl* had a strong stance on ethics (if you made it this far, you read a whole chapter about my problems with the biggest relationship on the show), but in the 2020s, given the social movements like #MeToo that have taken place since the original *Gossip Girl* ended, Kate being Gossip Girl, manipulating students and posting half-naked pictures of minors online, is an egregious abuse of power.

The *Gossip Girl* reboot was given so much more freedom to create more adult content because it was on a streamer, not a network like The CW, but perhaps watching it as an adult and knowing what I know now about the world versus what I knew in college is a bridge too far for enjoyment. It was canceled after two seasons.

But no matter how you felt about the reboot (I'm sorry, Josh Safran, don't be mad at me), one can't discount the fact that *Gossip Girl* was popular enough to warrant getting a second chance with a whole new cast of characters. And we can't forget another adjacent spinoff that *Gossip Girl* inspired—*NYC Prep*. *The O.C.* inspired MTV reality television (more like pseudo-scripted) phenomenon *Laguna Beach*, and *Gossip Girl* brought us an inside look into real-life Upper East Side teens on *NYC Prep*, which ran for only one season on Bravo. Turns out people don't want to watch real-life rich teens for more than like seven episodes.

Gossip Girl's Best Spinoff Is *NYC Prep*

Yeah, I know that *Gossip Girl* ended in 2012 and viewers had to wait nine years for the ill-fated *Gossip Girl* reboot. But what if I told you that the first addition to the *Gossip Girl* cinematic universe actually aired in 2009? That show, girls, gays, theys, and anyone else reading this book, is Bravo's *NYC Prep*.

Josh Schwartz and Stephanie Savage created *The O.C.* before they created *Gossip Girl*. *The O.C.* was pretty much an instant hit, with high ratings and favorability rankings that made it one of the most popular new dramas of the 2003–4 TV season. Of course, other people in Hollywood saw this popularity and wanted a chunk of it for themselves. In 2004, Liz Gateley created MTV's *Laguna Beach: The Real Orange County*, an IRL representation of the sexy, dramatic teenagers of Orange County, California. The show that gave us LC, Kristin Cavallari, Ste-phen, and so many memeable moments that are forever etched in the millennial lexicon.

But what a lot of people don't remember is that *Gossip Girl* inspired its own reality pseudo-spinoff, too. Debuting on June 23, 2009, *NYC Prep* followed a gaggle of actual rich kids from Manhattan (no Brooklynites here, but there was one who was considerably less well-off than the others) and their schedule of school, parties, shopping, charity events, and more.

The *NYC Prep* kids didn't exactly fit every archetype of the hot teens on *Gossip Girl*, but if we had to choose, Camille Hughes, a student at Professional Children's School, was the Blair Waldorf of the group. She was driven and dead set on attending an Ivy League School—Harvard, specifically. (She ended up attending the College of William & Mary.) She wore headbands. She didn't suffer fools. She was *really worried about the SAT, you guys.*

Jessie Leavitt went to the Dwight School on the Upper West Side (gross, gasp), and she was obsessed with her charity work with Operation Smile. She also loved fashion and talked about it incessantly. In that way she would be a combination of Jenny and Serena perhaps? She ended up going to the Fashion Institute of Technology in New York City. She had a crush on PC but he would never have a crush on her.

Kelli Tomashoff went to the Birch Wathen Lenox School on the Upper East Side, and she was an interesting case—she and her brother lived in an apartment in Manhattan, and her parents lived full-time in the Hamptons. Weird flex to leave your teens all alone in what is still their formative years, but OK! On the show, Kelli wants to be a pop singer, and a lot of her storyline revolves around making that happen. (It doesn't, but that's OK.)

Sebastian Oppenheim was probably the Nate of the group? He went to Ross School in East Hampton but was in Manhattan enough to be filmed as a student on *NYC Prep*. He had big, swoopy bangs that I absolutely would have been into when I was in high school, and he was always flinging them out of his eyes. All the girls thought he was the cutest. He liked every girl, ever.

Taylor DiGiovanni was the "poor" one of the group (and I say that very loosely), aka Dan Humphrey, because she went to Stuyvesant High School, a public school in Battery Park City, aka the lower end of Manhattan. Just a note though—Stuyvesant may be a New York City public school, but it is among the most selective high schools in New York City. It has rigorous academic admissions, and in some years it's harder to get into Stuyvesant than it is to get into Harvard. You can't buy your way in! A lot of *NYC Prep* was Taylor trying to figure out how she could fit in with the rich kids.

Peter Cary "PC" Peterson lived on the Upper West Side—again, the horror—and went to school with Jessie. His grandfather was a billionaire and a former US Secretary of Commerce. He was the Chuck Bass of the bunch, even down to the scarves. He had a casual insouciance to every situation—much like Chuck—and refused to take anything too seriously. Except be pretentious. He was good at that. Jessie loved him as more than a friend, but he did *not* want her as more than a friend. And maybe punching bag.

The cast of characters on *NYC Prep* was pretty interesting, but there were myriad reasons why the show just didn't work out and only lasted a season. First, these kids were not the hot twenty somethings-as-teens that we saw weekly on *Gossip Girl*. I'm not saying they were not attractive—but they weren't heading into their thirties and pretending they were late for homeroom. And because they were *actual teenagers*, there were all kinds of prohibitions about when and where Bravo could film their interactions. Filming was not allowed during school for any of the cast members, nor could any of the cast talk about their school specifically—none of the institutions wanted their names dragged through the mud for the sake of a reality show. Can you imagine the scandal?

Also, it's not like you could show these kids doing drugs or drinking or having sex or trying to open a burlesque club or doing anything that the *Gossip Girl* teens were doing in their fictional universe. There are laws around this. While, honestly, it was fun to watch Chuck and Blair and Georgina do their scheming all around the city, watching real-life kids try to hatch plans or play puppetry with their friends seemed . . . sociopathic almost? Entitled, definitely. With the fake love triangles and forced dinner parties, it almost bordered on being a part of the *Real Housewives* universe. It was simultaneously boring and a little immoral, but damn, was it fascinating from an anthropological standpoint. I felt sorry for them in a "it gets better" kind of way.

Where are the parents? Even Lily, who was the most neglectful parent on *Gossip Girl*, still at least lived with her kids. Kelli's parents were among the most shocking to me, because they let their, like, 15-year-old daughter live alone with her older brother? What if there had been an emergency? The Hamptons are two hours away *without* traffic from Manhattan, and that depends on which Hampton

THE END, THE REBOOT, AND BEYOND

you live in! East Hampton is at least 45 minutes further in traffic than Bridgehampton! Especially because Kelli wanted to be a singer. And as I sit writing this, watching more Hollywood sexual harassment and grooming scandals break, I can't believe Kelli's parents were comfortable with it. But I'm an old fuddy-duddy now, and I've seen too many true crime stories to look back.

It was also fascinating to watch the teenage cast members posture through their insecurities. My teenage years (and twenties . . . and thirties . . . wait . . .) were simply a series of years where I was trying to convince myself I was good enough, smart enough, and people loved me. On the outside, I seemed confident, but I had no idea what the fuck was going on. There's something endearing about watching continuing generations in that purgatory of not knowing who they are but, dear god, wanting to know ASAP. These teens were attending New York Fashion Week, going to "fancy" restaurants, going on vacation, having dog funerals, and modeling. They had all the money and opportunity in the world, and damn, they still didn't know how to get it together. It's endearing and charming, annoying and eye roll-inducing at the same time. And that's something that *Gossip Girl* didn't have—a soul.

In the end, the question stands: why is *Gossip Girl* still so popular? "No other show incorporated social media in the same way *Gossip Girl* did," Kelly Rutherford told *HURS* in 2023. "Everyone engages with social media now, and it's still a reflection of what we're dealing with as a society today as it relates to social media. It showcases the upsides and the downsides of everyone knowing what you're doing all the time. It was ahead of its time in that way."

"I think exactly what happened then is happening now and it has happened since the beginning of time," director Mark Piznarkski said. "To remake it in this day and age tomorrow, it would be the same show. There's nothing you'd have to change except use better phones. That kind of high school stuff is going to happen in perpetuity. That's just the way it is."

"It's a throwback and it's enjoyable, but I think [people] watch it cause it's still a really fun, smart show," said former *Gossip Girl* recapper and writer Chris Rovzar. "It's a show about people-watching. To have a show that is also very aware of the audience that's watching it because they're keeping track of these recaps and comments, it was very meta and it worked well."

"The thing that I think about with *Gossip Girl* is that, like, we really respected our audience," said writer and executive producer Amanda Lasher.

> We would like the literary references and the world of New York . . . we really cared about that. . . . We were not talking down to the

THE END, THE REBOOT, AND BEYOND

audience and that they were a part of it and that we were all in this thing together. It's also just so much fun, like the fun that we had writing the show, the deliciousness of it, I think, comes through.

Lasher continued:

Shows are shorter now, seasons are shorter, and you don't have as much time to invest in a character and in storylines. And I think that when you have a world that's so rich as *Gossip Girl* and there's so many episodes and you can really just, like, drop in. Good storytelling, incredible actors, beautiful sets, gorgeous costumes, great writing, well produced. It has a timelessness about it . . . there's a genuineness to the work that people did. And I think that the show itself stands the test of time.

Nicole Fiscella, who played Izzy, thinks the shows endure because people want to revisit their youth whenever they want. "I think that teenagers gravitate towards [these shows] because they're like, oh, this is actually real, right? This is actually what's happening, not, you know, not in all the ways of *Gossip Girl*, of course . . . [they think], oh, this actually can be very similar to my life and they can identify with it," she told me. "And then I think older people want to feel young again. We want to be like, that's all we need to worry about. We don't need to think about the bigger things in the world. Everything that feels just so heavy. It's sort of nice to be able to have something light."

"We don't really make media for teens anymore! *Gossip Girl* was that like, I hate to say old-fashioned, but like that good, old fashioned, 23-episode season formula. You can experiment . . . and you're writing as the season is airing, so you can react in real time to whatever's happening," writer Tyler McCall said.

McCall makes an interesting point here, too, because so many of the shows, like *Gossip Girl*, that people choose as "comfort" shows—you know, the ones that you like to just have in the background while you're cleaning, sleeping, working, scrolling, existing—are those older, full-season, episodic shows. Not every episode of a 24-episode season is a winner. There are filler episodes, there are capsule episodes, there are ones you can skip. With today's tighter, ten-episode seasons of shows, a viewer is forced to be on while they're watching. The odds are higher, and you have to pay attention. It's hard to zone out. Perhaps teen TV of yore also remains popular because you can just bliss out while you're watching, kind of like you did when you were an actual teenager and had far fewer responsibilities.

Of course, we also just want to watch hot people do bad things, too. "I think every once in a while [the teen drama] goes out of fashion, and people rediscover it like, oh, right, we love watching people figure out who they are and maturing . . . People love remembering their own messy youth and seeing a better version of it, because they're always a better version of it," journalist and *Gossip Girl* recapper Jessica Pressler said. "They're always wearing better clothes, and they always are more articulate, even when they're messy. It's nostalgic for grown-ups and I think we just like to watch people evolve."

Weiss said people want something to comfort them during their everyday lives. "They're looking for clues that Dan was Gossip Girl," Weiss joked. "I think there's this propulsive quality to the show that makes you want to keep watching episode after episode," she continued. "For many people it is still a comfort watch, as are the other shows in this genre, as something that people put on before they go to bed or while they're doing dishes or laundry. It's just their thing in their life that they want to have."

Szadkowski said *Gossip Girl* is still a hit because it's equal parts aspirational and nostalgic.

> The teen genre makes so much sense because the time when you feel your feelings to the fullest and the day-to-day stakes of life are the highest. And it's, you know, before life kind of beats you down and before the responsibilities of adulthood change your priorities . . . [there are] issues of identity and like, love, betrayal, you know, the great the, the extent to which humans, you know, need and want and push and pull each other is the most in those formative years. Even as older people, I think we are drawn to remember ourselves in that time, and we're drawn to watch drama unfold in that time because things mean more to people in that phase of life. . . . Everybody's better looking and has better clothes, but the same feelings.

Though the nature of television and how we consume media has changed, there is something eternal about the teen drama. Youth culture is pop culture. The idea of turning back the clock, of wanting to go back to a time of less responsibility, of more fun, of when life hadn't quite made a mess of us yet, is universal. If being a teen is about wistfulness and yearning, watching teens on TV means we can relive that wistfulness any time we'd like. There are definitive benefits to being an adult, but who wants to be an adult all the time? Ultimately, *Gossip Girl*'s enduring popularity isn't about the money, clothes, and cars but the love,

New York City Mayor Michael Bloomberg delivers a Mayoral Proclamation celebrating the 100th episode of *Gossip Girl*, accompanied by Kelly Rutherford, Blake Lively, Penn Badgley, and Matthew Settle. Bloomberg would go on to make a cameo in the series finale, reacting to the news of Gossip Girl's true identity. It was Dan, but he thought it was Dorota.

Photo by Jonathon Ziegler/Patrick McMullan via Getty Images.

friendship, promise, and potential that exists in your formative years. Wondering what could have been has a temporary salve in the form of our favorite comforting, escapist television, and if it takes place in a limo with plenty of champagne? All the better.

Gossip Girl: Where Are They Now?

The last episode of *Gossip Girl* ended with a five-year time jump, but since it's been a good thirteen years since the finale and nearly a decade since the flash-forward, I thought it prudent to explore where I think the characters would be in 2026 and beyond.

Serena Van Der Woodsen

Serena and Dan's wedding and the #MeToo movement drummed up new interest in Dan's time as Gossip Girl, with the pair facing online scrutiny (especially on Twitter) that Serena was suffering from Stockholm Syndrome because she married a man who sold her secrets. The two decamped to Southampton permanently to get away from NYC's prying eyes. They have 7-year-old twins, a son and a daughter, both blond, to Dan's chagrin, that attend the Ross School in Bridgehampton. Serena sits on the board of a handful of various Hamptons charities, and she has a dedicated following on Instagram and TikTok of 28 million and 14 million people, respectively. Her posts are mostly OOTDs.

Dan Humphrey

Dan and Serena are still married. He sold his second book in 2019, a gender-swapped retelling of *Beowulf*, to Nate's new *Spectator* book imprint (Nate bought the book as a favor to Dan), and it crashed and burned, not even close to hitting *The New York Times* Best Seller list. Now a frustrated artist with family (aka his wife's) money, Dan spends the bulk of his day in his usual corner at the American Hotel in Sag Harbor "writing," which mostly means filling black hardcover Leuchtturm1917 notebooks with gibberish from his Montblanc fountain pen (he thinks having to fill the ink is more authentic to the writing experience).

Blair Waldorf

Blair and Chuck had another child, Jacqueline (named in memory of Chuck's Uncle Jack, who died in 2018 in a tragic scuba diving accident) in 2019. The now family of four, including their first child, Henry, still live in the Upper East Side townhouse seen in the series finale. Blair remains the creative lead for Waldorf Designs, and though her collections aren't seen as particularly groundbreaking, they're very popular with the Regency-to-Mar-a-Lago set, and Blair does very well with them. Blair is currently developing plans to branch out into home design, kitchenware, and more, with the hopes that she'll be a younger, more affluent, less aggressive Martha Stewart.

Chuck Bass

Chuck is still running Bass Industries, and he's also purchased a number of New York City apartment buildings and converted their units into illegal Airbnbs. (He figures he can't beat Airbnb, so he might as well join them.) Chuck was embroiled in a 2021 scandal with an OnlyFans model, but he and Blair worked through it. He is still required to share his location with Blair at all times.

Eleanor Waldorf and Cyrus Rose

Eleanor and Cyrus are still married and living in their townhouse on the Upper East Side, rarely journeying below 59th Street—Bloomingdale's is the southern border. They became a viral sensation, just like Ina and Jeffrey Garten, during the Covid-19 pandemic in 2020 because of Eleanor's unhinged Instagram Lives where she drank giant gin martinis (very dry with a twist), sang show tunes with

Cyrus as accompaniment on piano, and gossiped about the people she hated in the fashion industry. Wealthy in their own right, they're both even richer after selling Waldorf Designs to LVMH for $348 million in 2022.

Nate Archibald

That mayoral run Nate hinted to in the series finale? He ran for mayor but ended up losing to Michael Bloomberg, who decided to throw his hat in the ring for a fourth term. Nate settled for New York City Comptroller, where he quickly used the embezzlement skills his father taught him to skim money off the top of the city's coffers during the chaos of the Covid-19 pandemic. With rumors of an audit and investigation from Attorney General Tish James pending, Nate resigned as Comptroller, citing health issues, and went back to *The New York Spectator*, which is now a full-scale media company with a publishing house and cable news. He's still biding his time, planning on making Michael Bloomberg "pay," whatever that means.

Jenny Humphrey

Jenny moved to Paris in 2018 to start an eponymous fashion label. In 2019, she was hired to assist Demna Gvasalia at Balenciaga, but when she got into a tiff with Kim

Kardashian before the Met Gala, she was let go. She's now the Creative Director at Givenchy, making her one of only a few female leads of a major fashion brand. She has a cat and a long-term partner, Val, a Parisian, who she met when he scolded her for taking her *café au lait* to go.

Vanessa Abrams

Vanessa is a community activist and political organizer with 9 million followers on TikTok. She lives in Alphabet City and pretends to be a leftist vegan, but sometimes, you can find her eating a double cheeseburger at the 7th Street Burger in the East Village. She goes at 2:00 a.m. (they close at 3:00 a.m.) when no one will be sober enough to notice who she is and what she's doing. She is becoming more politically moderate as she ages, but that is a bigger secret than her love for griddled beef patties, because she doesn't want to lose followers. She is single.

Rufus Humphrey

Rufus and Lisa Loeb (always two names) are still going strong. They left New York City in the 2020 pandemic because they just couldn't stand to "see their city like this" and now spend most of their time on a ranch in Taos, New Mexico. Rufus wears a lot of turquoise jewelry, and it suits him. Rufus writes musical scores for shows like *Yellowstone*, and he and Lisa Loeb are working on their third folk album together under the band name Lincoln Loeb.

Lily Van Der Woodsen

Lily is still with William, the father of her children, but she refuses to marry him again. She doesn't trust him because he lied and told her she had cancer all those years ago. Lily's life hasn't changed all that much since 2017, minus the elevator mirror selfie she takes every morning for her Instagram followers. She does love to show off her Birkin collection.

Eric Van Der Woodsen

Eric doesn't speak to anyone from his young life except for Jenny. He lives in Prenzlauer Berg, Berlin, with his partner, Klaus, and their three dachshunds.

Georgina Sparks

In 2017, with the help of a good crisis PR team, Georgina and Jack Bass rebranded themselves to be the second coming of JFK, Jr. and Carolyn Bessette. When Jack died in 2018,

Georgina took this as an opportunity for another rebrand, this time as grieving wife Jackie Kennedy. Unfortunately, this new cache and all of Jack's inherited money and shares didn't get her what she ultimately wanted—an apartment at 740 Park Avenue. She is still plotting how to get her dream real estate.

Dorota Kishlovsky

Dorota and Vanya live in the Upper East Side townhouse next to Chuck and Blair—a gift from the Waldorfs—with their three children. Everyone moves freely between the two homes. It's slightly chaotic with five kids running back and forth, but Blair secretly prefers it to her stuffy, only-child upbringing. Vanya takes care of the properties, and Dorota also runs a thriving nanny/housekeeping agency to find quality help for new generations of wealthy Upper East Siders.

Bart Bass

He's still dead. No one misses him.

Gossip Girl: Where Are They Now: Real-Life Edition

Now that we know how (possibly, probably) the characters from *Gossip Girl* are doing in the present-day world, why don't we check in on what the *Gossip Girl* players have been up to?

Blake Lively

High: Wore a lot of suits in *A Simple Favor*, appeared in the Lonely Island video for "I Just Had Sex" on SNL, married Deadpool, attended the Super Bowl with Taylor Swift, directed Taylor Swift's video for "I Bet You Think About Me."

Low: Starred in *Green Lantern* (but at least that's where she met her husband?), fought against the paparazzi because they keep trying to publish pictures of her children (this is not a blow against her, more that it's insane she has to keep fighting for them to leave her family alone).

Oh No: Adopted a thick Boston accent for *The Town*, tried to start a *Goop*-adjacent lifestyle website, *Preserve*, that she closed because, as she told *Vogue*, it was "not making a difference in people's lives, whether superficially or in a meaningful way."

Leighton Meester

High: Sang with Gabe Saporta and Cobra Starship on "Good Girls Go Bad" (this was way before *Gossip Girl* wrapped, but I'm an emo kid so let me celebrate), starred on *Single Parents* on ABC, became Mrs. Seth Cohen, made her Broadway debut in *Of Mice and Men* in 2014, *Life Partners* with Gillian Jacobs.

Low: *EXmas* with Robbie Amell . . . it wasn't . . . great. Even for the "holiday romance" genre. (Sorry Leighton ILY), her being extremely private because I love her and want to know more about her adorable family even though she's entitled to her privacy.

Oh No: The *Nashville*-adjacent movie *Country Strong*, *Monte Carlo* with Selena Gomez and Katie Cassidy, *That's My Boy*, yes, the Adam Sandler movie.

Chace Crawford

High: Landing the role of The Deep on *The Boys* and *Gen V*.

Low: His role in *What to Expect When You're Expecting*, a lot of other movies that seem like they went straight to video because I have literally never heard of any of them.

Oh No: One singular episode of *Glee* (the series' 100th!), where he played Biff, Quinn Fabray's new boyfriend.

Penn Badgley

High: Turning Dan Humphrey into a franchise, because Joe Goldberg from *You* is basically just an older, highly escalated version of Dan as Gossip Girl, his *Podcrushed* podcast, all of his lip syncing TikToks, his role in *Easy A*.

Low: Breaking up with Zoë Kravitz (I completely forgot they dated), *The Stepfather* with the guy from *Nip/Tuck* and Amber Heard.

Oh No: Honestly, Penn's been crushing it. Good for him.

Ed Westwick

High: His *PEOPLE* spread after marrying Amy Jackson in Italy, still being BFF with Kelly Rutherford, *White Gold* on BBC Two.

Low: Being accused of alleged sexual assault by multiple women (the Los Angeles District Attorney dropped the charges due to a lack of evidence), *Chalet Girl*.

Oh No: Crime drama *Wicked City*, which only lasted three episodes on ABC, the TV version of Guy Ritchie's *Snatch*.

Michelle Trachtenberg

High: Making that money through voice work on shows like *Robot Chicken*—we love when there's no hair and makeup needed.

Low: Assorted made-for-TV movies that didn't make much of a splash, *Mercy*.

Oh No: Appearing for two episodes on the *Gossip Girl* reboot. Sadly, this was one of her final on-screen appearances before her death in 2025 from complications from diabetes.

Taylor Momsen

High: Living her dream as the lead singer of the Pretty Reckless since 2009, quitting acting because it wasn't her true passion anymore.

Low: A period of too much eyeliner.

Oh No: Nothing here, honestly. Momsen listened to her heart because she didn't want to be Cindy Lou Who anymore.

Jessica Szohr

High: *Piranha 3D, Shameless,* her *Gossip Girl*-driven *XOXO with Jessica Szohr* podcast, *Two Night Stand*.

Low: Being on an episode of *Punk'd* as the punk-er and not the punk-ee. (I think pranks are mean, sue me.)

Oh No: A quick foray into Hallmark-adjacent Christmas movies.

Matthew Settle

High: Appearing on Broadway in *Chicago: The Musical* in 2010.

Low: The 2014 movie *Ouija*.

Oh No: Disappearing off the face of the earth. Minus one episode of *Criminal Minds: Beyond Borders*, Settle has done *no TV* since *Gossip Girl*. Man, where you at?

Connor Paolo

High: Playing Declan on ABC's *Revenge* alongside Emily Van Camp. Another iconic dramatic mess of a show.

Low: More like lower-budget—lots of releases that didn't hit the mainstream. (That's ok, because they can't all be blockbusters.)

Oh No: A horror movie with Jonathan Bennett, aka Aaron Samuels from *Mean Girls*, set on New York's Fire Island.

Kelly Rutherford

High: Being even more famous for elevator mirror selfies on Instagram, roles on *Quantico* and the *Dynasty* reboot.

Low: An absolutely brutal, $2 million, years-long divorce complete with a bitter custody case concerning her very young children.

Oh No: A role on *Pretty Little Liars: The Perfectionists*. We don't do reboots around here, Kelly!

Selected References

Bindig, Lori (2014), *Gossip Girl: A Critical Understanding*. Lanham, MD: Lexington Books.

Bricker, Tierney (2021), "You Know You Still Love It: How Gossip Girl Defied Expectations to Define a Generation." *E! News*, July 4. https://www.eonline.com/news/1057823/you-know-you-still-love-it-how-gossip-girl-defied-expectations-to-define-a-generation

Bruce, Leslie and Lacey Rose (2012), "The Birth (and Death?) of 'Gossip Girl'." *The Hollywood Reporter*, January 24. https://www.hollywoodreporter.com/tv/tv-news/birth-death-gossip-girl-284593/

Carlson, Meghan (2009), "Interview: Producer Josh Safran on Everything 'Gossip Girl'." *BuddyTV*. September 8. https://www.buddytv.com/interview-producer-josh-safran-on-everything-gossip-girl/

"Chace Crawford" (2023), *Podcrushed*, October 5.

SELECTED REFERENCES

Craighead, Olivia (2024), "Who Did Chace Crawford Hook up with on Gossip Girl?" *The Cut*, June 13. https://www.thecut.com/article/who-did-chace-crawford-hook-up-with-gossip-girl.html

"David Rapaport" (2022), *XOXO with Jessica SZOHR. iHeartRadio* app. February 2.

DeSantis, Rachel (2023), "Gossip Girl Cast: Where Are They Now?" *Entertainment Weekly*, January 23. https://ew.com/tv/gossip-girl-then-and-now/

Duboff, Josh (2017), "When Gossip Girl Ruled the World." *Vanity Fair*. August 30. https://www.vanityfair.com/hollywood/2017/08/gossip-girl-ten-year-anniversary

"Ed Westwick" (2022), *XOXO with Jessica SZOHR. iHeartRadio* app. February 2.

"Ed Westwick Talks about Chuck & Blair, His Character's Evolution, Chace Crawford & Gossip Girl" (2024), *FR Conventions*, April 18.

Exton, Emily (2022), "Gossip Girl: The Best of Chuck and Blair," *Entertainment Weekly*, August 12. https://ew.com/gallery/gossip-girl-best-chuck-blair/

Fiscella, Nicole (2024), Personal interview. September 26.

Frischer, Brooke (2024), "How I Shop: Kelly Rutherford." *Fashionista*, March 7. https://fashionista.com/2024/03/kelly-rutherford-fashion-style-interview

SELECTED REFERENCES

Gay, Jason (2009), "'Gossip Girl': Dirty Pretty Things." *Rolling Stone*, April 2. https://www.rollingstone.com/tv-movies/tv-movie-news/gossip-girl-dirty-pretty-things-184242/

"Gossip Girl's Music Supervisor on Creating the Show's Soundtrack" (2008), *Vanity Fair*, May 12. https://www.vanityfair.com/news/2008/05/gossip-girls-mu?srsltid=AfmBOoqc9tgK3qfDdIju5Rh6syP9JF8mjrMvWCfQI2Nq9PfAhzGcqyzv

"'Gossip Girl': The Steamy Rolling Stone Cover Shoot with Terry Richardson" (2009), *Rolling Stone*, March 18. https://www.rollingstone.com/music/music-lists/gossip-girl-the-steamy-rolling-stone-cover-shoot-with-terry-richardson-206695/

Halterman, Jim (2009), "Interview: *Gossip Girl* Executive Producer Stephanie Savage," *The Futon Critic*, March 13.

Herman, Alison (2017), "How 'Gossip Girl' Shaped the CW," *The Ringer*, September 19. https://www.theringer.com/2017/09/19/tv/gossip-girl-cw-ten-year-anniversary

Iandoli, Kathy (2012), "Alexandra Patsavas Makes the Soundtrack to Your Life," *VICE*, November 6. https://www.vice.com/en/article/alexandra-patsavas-makes-the-soundtrack-to-your-life/

"Josh Schwartz & Stephanie Savage Vol. 1" (2022), *XOXO with Jessica SZOHR*, iHeartRadio app. January 18.

"Josh Schwartz & Stephanie Savage Vol. 2" (2022), *XOXO with Jessica SZOHR*, iHeartRadio app. February 9.

Jung, E. Alex (2017), "The 'Gossip Girl' Creators Look Back at What Never Made It to Air." *Vulture*. September 19. https://

SELECTED REFERENCES

www.vulture.com/2017/09/gossip-girl-creators-what-never-made-it-to-air.html

Kinane, Ruth (2021), "Gossip Girl Showrunner Explains How the New Series Is Different from the Original," *Entertainment Weekly*, June 7. https://ew.com/tv/gossip-girl-showrunner-joshua-safran-preview/

La Ferla, Ruth (2008), "Forget Gossip, Girl; the Buzz Is About the Clothes." *New York Times*, July 8. https://www.nytimes.com/2008/07/08/fashion/08gossip.html

Lasher, Amanda (2024), Personal interview, September 30.

McCall, Tyler (2024). Personal interview, September 17.

McCall, Tyler (2017), "Reflecting on a Decade of 'Gossip Girl' with Eric Daman." *Fashionista*. November 14. https://fashionista.com/2017/08/gossip-girl-fashion-style-clothes-eric-daman

"Michelle Trachtenberg" (2022), *XOXO with Jessica SZOHR. iHeartRadio* app. March 23.

Moore, Julia (2024), "Chace Crawford Was 'Blasé' about Gossip Girl Audition after Friday Night Lights Rejection: 'Devastated'," *PEOPLE*, June 12. https://people.com/chace-crawford-was-blase-at-gossip-girl-audition-after-friday-night-lights-rejection-8662100?

Nesvig, Kara K. (2019), "'Gossip Girl' Writer Reveals Dan Humphrey Wasn't the Original Gossip Girl," *Teen Vogue*, November 12. https://www.teenvogue.com/story/dan-humphrey-not-original-gossip-girl

SELECTED REFERENCES

Neumann, Sean (2017), "How the Music Supervisor for 'The O.C.' and 'Gossip Girl' Changed the Game for Indie Rock," *VICE*, October 20. https://www.vice.com/en/article/music-supervisor-alexandra-patsavas-interview-2017-the-oc-gossip-girl-tvweek/

Odell, Amy (2011), "The Gossip Girl Clothing Line Is Coming," *The Cut*, September 16. https://www.thecut.com/2011/09/the_gossip_girl_clothing_line.html

Piznarski, Mark (2024), Personal interview. September 28.

Pressler, Jessica (2024), Personal interview. September 16.

"Pret-A-Poor J with Amanda Lasher" (2022), *XOXO with Jessica SZOHR. iHeartRadio* app. May 25.

r/GossipGirl (2025, January 6), *Reddit*. https://www.reddit.com/r/GossipGirl/

Rivera, Jeff. "So What Do You Do, Cecily von Ziegesar, Creator of Gossip Girl?" *Mediabistro*. https://www.mediabistro.com/interviews/so-what-do-you-do-cecily-von-ziegesar-creator-of-gossip-girl/

Rovzar, Chris (2024), Personal interview. September 18.

Rubin, Julia (2012), "Kate Moss, Audrey Hepburn, and Designer Headbands: How Gossip Girl Became TV's 'Fashion Monster'," *Teen Vogue*, December 18. https://www.teenvogue.com/gallery/gossip-girl-style-eric-daman

"Sebastian Stan" (2023), *Podcrushed*, August 31.

"Sebastian Stan" (2024), *Variety*, September 19.

SELECTED REFERENCES

Soo Hoo, Fawnia (2018), "For TV Costume Designers, Borrowing from Fashion Houses Hasn't Been Easy," *Fashionista*, January 9. https://fashionista.com/2018/01/tv-costume-design-borrowing-clothes

"Stephanie Savage, TV Producer and Co-Creator of *Gossip Girl*" (2023), *The Selfish Gift*. April 12.

Szadkowski, Zuzanna (2024), Personal interview, September 17.

"Taylor Momsen" (2023), *Podcrushed*, September 7.

"The Influence: Kelly Rutherford." *Luminaire*. https://luminaireco.com/articles/the-influence-kelly-rutherford

"The Nasty Thrill of 'Gossip Girl': On the Set of TV's Hottest Show in *Rolling Stone*" (2009), *Rolling Stone*, March 18. https://www.rollingstone.com/culture/culture-news/the-nasty-thrill-of-gossip-girl-on-the-set-of-tvs-hottest-show-in-rolling-stone-65825/

Travis, Emlyn (2023), "Taylor Momsen Says 'Complicated' Decision to Leave *Gossip Girl* Changed Her Life 'Overnight'," *Entertainment Weekly*, September 7. https://ew.com/tv/taylor-momsen-says-leaving-gossip-girl-changed-life-overnight/

"VIDEO: Interview with JaNeika and JaSheika James of the 'Gossip Girl' Spinoff" (2021), *TeenDramaWhore*, February 24. https://teendramawhore.substack.com/p/janeika-jasheika-james-interview-gossip-girl

Ward, Kate (2009), "Parents Television Council Writes Letter Criticizing Threesome Storyline on 'Gossip Girl',"

SELECTED REFERENCES

Entertainment Weekly, November 3. https://ew.com/article/2009/11/03/parents-television-council-gossip-girl/

Watson, Shyla (2019), "Gossip Girl Was Actually Supposed to Be Nate, not Dan, and Now It All Makes Sense," *Buzzfeed*, November 11. https://www.buzzfeed.com/shylawatson/gossip-girl-actually-nate-not-dan

Weiss, Shari (2024), Personal interview. September 19.

Weiss, Shari (2025, January 6), *Teen Drama Whore*. https://substack.com/@teendramawhore

Westenfeld, Adrienne (2021), "Cecily Von Ziegesar Is Glad the Gossip Girl 2.0 Characters 'Give a Sh*t'," July 20. https://www.esquire.com/entertainment/books/a37048792/cecily-von-ziegesar-gossip-girl-reboot-interview/

White, Abbey (2021), "'Gossip Girl' Actress Yin Chang Says Character Was Rewritten into Asian Stereotype on CW Series," *The Hollywood Reporter*, August 13. https://www.hollywoodreporter.com/tv/tv-news/cw-gossip-girl-yin-chang-nelly-yuki-asian-american-representatinon-hbo-max-1234997643/

Wyatt, Edward (2009), "'Gossip Girl' Episode Draws Criticism from Parents' Group," *New York Times*, November 4. https://archive.nytimes.com/mediadecoder.blogs.nytimes.com/2009/11/04/gossip-girl-episode-draws-criticism-from-parents-group/

Acknowledgments

Writing about celebrities is way easier than writing about and thanking the people in your real life, but I'm filled with such gratitude in the production of this book that I'm going to try anyway.

To my agent extraordinaire, Amanda Bernardi, your brilliant direction and pep talks gave me the energy and the courage to cut out all the imposter syndrome and write it already! I can't wait to see what else we'll do together, and I hope I'm still the only client who, when adding invites to your online calendar, calls them "SPIRALING" and nothing else. Here's to being tall and blonde and reading too much.

Speaking of being tall and blonde, to Blake Lively: thanks for being my forever hair inspiration.

To Chris Chappell, Emily Burr, Barbara Claire, Jane Fieldsend, Anne Hunt, Jessica Thwaite, Carey Cameron, Meghan McDonagh, Shereen Muhyeddeen, and the rest of the

ACKNOWLEDGMENTS

team at Bloomsbury, thank you so much for sharing my vision with this project. I'm so thankful for your guidance.

To Nicole Pomarico and Martha Sorren, journalistic colleagues and *Bachelor* coverage buddies turned BFFs, thank you for your keen editing eyes, literary encouragement, and answering every "do you think I should . . ." question thrown in the group chat. Two out of three of us are now published authors, so all I can say is: Martha, your turn.

To Kait Franssen, Nicole Mohammadi, Kristen Roberts, Shelbi Thurau, Emily Stone, and Sarah Wolff, there's a line from *Freaks and Geeks* that says, "I don't need another friend. I already have two." Luckily, I have many more times that amount! Your longstanding, unconditional friendship has gotten me through every moment, especially when I was particularly salty (and salty is an understatement) about being on deadline. Thank you for listening and sharing plenty of platters of appetizers, always.

To Taylor Marie, Mom, and Dad, my first collective sounding board and cheerleading section, thank you for listening to my stories (did you know I was going to be a writer, or . . .?) and allowing me to destroy you all at Jeopardy! I wouldn't be where I am today without you.

To Henry, thanks for always letting me be me, no matter what I wanted to do next. And also, thanks for listening to me rant about Blair and Chuck when you didn't know what I was talking about. I love you.

Index

Italic page numbers indicate illustrations.
Characters are filed by their first name eg. Blair Waldorf not Waldorf, Blair. Real-life people are filed by their surname eg. Badgley, Penn.

Aaron Rose, Serena and 136
addict Dad storyline, Nate's 65
adults, casting 30–2, *32*
age differential in sex 123–4, 125–6
Agnes Andrews 140
annoying characters 138–40

Badgley, Penn
    after *Gossip Girl* 216
    casting as Dan Humphrey 32–3
    on dating other cast members 128–9
    on fame, end of show and 79–80

fashion, viewers' buying patterns and 169
    at Teen Choice Awards *64*
    100th episode *206*
    see also Dan Humphrey
Banks, Tyra 92
Bart Bass 104
    in 2025 213
    as annoying character 140
"Believe" (The Bravery) 180
Beverly Hills 90210 1–2
Bilson, Rachel 92
Blair Waldorf
    in 2025 208–9

INDEX

casting of Leighton
    Meester 26–7
character arc 143
Chuck, unhealthy relationship
    with 141–55, *155*
Dan, relationship with 156
fashion, *Gossip Girl*
    and 163–4
Louis, relationship with 159
sex on *Gossip Girl* 121–2
virginity, loss of 121–2
Bloomberg, Michael 94, *206*
books, *Gossip Girl* 16–18, 20–1
bus tours to sets/actors' hang out
    spots 78–9

camera phones, lack of 84–5
campiness, lack of in reboot 193
Captain Archibald, casting of
    Sam Robards 29–30
Carter Baizen, casting of
    Sebastian Stan 31
casting
  adults 30–2, *32*
  Blair/Leighton Meester 26–7
  Carter Baizen/Sebastian
    Stan 31
  chemistry 33–4

Chuck/Ed Westwick 25–6
Dan Humphrey/Penn
    Badgley 32–3
Dorota/Zuzanna
    Szadkowski 30
Georgina Sparks/Michelle
    Trachtenberg 32
Howard "the Captain"
    Archibald/Sam
    Robards 29–30
Isabel/Nicole Fiscella
    28–9
Jenny/Taylor Momsen
    24–5
Lily Van Der Woodsen/Kelly
    Rutherford 31
Nate/Chace Crawford 27
Serena/Blake Lively 23–4
Vanessa/Jessica Szohr 28
Catherine, relationship with
    Nate 156–7
cell phones, use of in series 38
Chang, Yin 98–9, 100
characters
  annoying 138–40
  diversity, lack of 96–103
  real-life spinoff *NYC Prep*
    197–201

INDEX

softness of interpersonal
    relationships   49
writing for   48–51
see also individual characters
Chuck Bass
    in 2025   209
    Blair, unhealthy relationship
        with   141–55, *155*
    in the books   45
    casting of Ed Westwick   25–6
    clothes   166–7
    Elle and the Secret Society
        storyline   65
    as gay character   104–6
    as hypersexualized   124–5
    Jenny, relationship with   157–8
    pilot episode   39
    sexual assaults by   124
    as sexually aggressive   143
    trading Blair for father's hotel
        storyline   67
Chung, Alexa   93
Cleavage Rhombus   58–9
clothes
    online feedback on *Gossip Girl*
        58–9
    see also fashion, *Gossip Girl*
        and

Colin, relationship with
    Serena   158
commentators via Daily Intel
    blog   52–62
costumes
    online feedback on
        Gossip Girl   58–9
    see also fashion, *Gossip Girl*
        and
Crawford, Chace
    after *Gossip Girl*   215–16
    casting as Nate   27
    fans on sets and   73, 74
    first meeting with Leighton   27
    media stories about   107
    on set   *132*
    at Teen Choice Awards   *64*
    see also Nate Archibald
cultural significance of *Gossip*
    Girl   7
CW   15
Cyrus Rose in 2025   209–10

Daily Intel blog   52–62
Daman, Eric   58–9, 161–73, 194
Dan Humphrey
    in 2025   208
    Blair, relationship with   156

INDEX

in the books 45
casting of Penn Badgley 32–3
Georgina's faux baby
 storyline 66
Olivia, relationship
 with 158–9
pilot episode 39
publication in *The New Yorker*
 storyline 66–7
revealed as Gossip Girl 68–9,
 184–90
secret sibling of Serena and
 Dan 64–5
Serena and 137
sex and 125–6
"Dark on Fire" (Turin
 Brakes) 181
details of new York, attention
 to 46
DiGiovanni, Taylor 198–9
diversity
 characters, lack of
  regarding 96–103
 LGBTQ representation 103–6
 New York, people of color
  in 95
 reboot 100–3
 1990s/2000s 14

1960s/1970s television 12–13
in teen dramas, lack of 95–6
tokenism 96
women on the show 106–11
Dorota Kishlovsky
 in 2025 213
 casting of Zuzanna
  Szadkowski 30
 comforting Blair 49, 63,
  189–90
 first appearance of 49
double standard, male/female
 cast members 106–10

Easter egging 46–7
Ehrenreich, Alden 33
Eleanor Waldorf in 2025
 209–10
Elle and the Secret Society
 storyline 65
end of *Gossip Girl*
 fame and 79–80
 final episode 184–90
 flashforward to 2017 185
 Gossip Girl, Dan revealed as
  184–90
 spinoff *NYC Prep*
  196–201

INDEX

storylines previous to 183–4
see also reboot
episodes per season 183, 184, 192, 204
Eric Van Der Woodsen
   in 2025 212
   gay plotline with 103–4
Euphoria, comparison with *Gossip Girl* 126–7

fame
   camera phones, lack of 84–5
   celebrities wanting to meet cast members 85
   end of show and 79–80
   fast-rise, impact on actors 81–4
   perks of 84
   relationships between actors 82–3
familial collapse/addict Dad storyline, Nate's 65
fans
   Blair/Chuck relationship, reactions to 150–1
   commentators via Daily Intel blog 52–62
   Paris, 2010 85–7, *91*

scripts, leaks of 80–1
   on sets 73–80
   social media, beginnings of 71–2
   social media communication by 72–3
   spoilers and 80
   writers' strike, 2007–2008 71
fashion, *Gossip Girl* and
   author's experience 161–2
   Blair 163–4
   Daman, Eric, costume designer 161–73
   Gossip Girl fashion line, lack of 170–1
   'inspired by' looks 171–2
   Lily 166
   menswear 166–7
   network pushback 168–9
   reboot 194
   retail landscape, impact on 172–3
   school uniform 168, *177*
   Upper East Side schools, inspiration from 167
   viewers' buying patterns and 169–70
fat phobia in 2000s 142

INDEX

faux baby storyline   66
feedback on *Gossip Girl*
　online   52–62
　see also fans
female friendships   106–11
female masturbation   129–30
final episode   184–90
Fiscella, Nicole
　casting as Isabel   28–9
　enduring popularity of *Gossip Girl*   203
　fast-rise fame and   83
　as person of color   97–8
　see also Isabel
flashforward to 2017   185
FOX, beginnings of   13
friendships between women   106–11
fun, *Gossip Girl* as   47–8

Gateley, Liz   197
gay characters   103–6
Georgina Sparks
　in 2025   212–13
　casting of Michelle Trachtenberg   32
　crew ganging up on storyline   66

faux baby storyline   66
Go Piss Girl meme   112–13, *114*
Gossip Girl (narrator) in pilot episode   37
Gossip Girl (persona)
　Dan revealed as   68–9, 184–90
　Kate Keller as in reboot   195
Gossip Girl (show)
　author's experience   3–4
　books   16–18, 20–1
　early reception of   41–3
　enduring popularity of   202–7
　first season promotion   *16*
　impact on television and culture   190
　marketing image for first season   *35*
　origins and development of   16–22
　pilot episode   *8*, 36–9
　previous attempts to screen   19
　themes of   49
　writers' strike, 2007–2008   43
gravitas as missing in reboot   192
guest stars   92–4

234

INDEX

hair
  Blake Lively, casting of   24
  Leighton Meester, casting of   24
  pilot episode   39
Haskins, Rick   44, 45, 72–3
Hilton, Perez   142
Howard "the Captain" Archibald, casting of Sam Robards   29–30
Hughes, Camille   197
hypersexualized, Chuck as   124–5

influencer, Serena Van Der Woodsen as   6
insider references   46–7
Internet
  Gossip Girl and   4–7
  recaps and feedback on *Gossip Girl*   52–62
interpersonal relationships, softness of   49
Isabel
  casting of Nicole Fiscella   28–9
  see also Fiscella, Nicole
Ivy, relationship with Rufus   158

James, JaNeika   100–2
James, JaSheika   100–1, 102
Jenny Humphrey
  in 2025   210–11
  as annoying character   138
  casting of Taylor Momsen   24–5
  change of story due to exit of Momsen   49–51
  Chuck, relationship with   157–8
  parenting, lack of   123
  sex and   123
Johnson, Jennifer   74

Kate Keller as Gossip Girl in reboot   195

Lady Gaga   93
Laguna Beach: The Real Orange County   197
Lasher, Amanda   45–6, 48–9, 56, 57, 60, 97, 110, 111, 129–30, 176, 188–9, 202–3
Lauper, Cyndi   92
Leavitt, Jessie   197–8
Lepore, Nanette   171–2

INDEX

LGBTQ representation 103–6
Lily Van Der Woodsen
   in 2025 212
   casting of Kelly
      Rutherford 31
   as parent 104, 117, 119–21, 135
   wedding 51–2
Lively, Blake
   after *Gossip Girl* 214
   casting as Serena 23–4
   on dating other cast members 128
   fame, relationships between actors and 82–3
   fans on set 78
   fashion, *Gossip Girl* and 164–6
   possibility of reboot, reaction to 190
   Rolling Stone photoshoot 127–8
   rumors about friendships between cast members 106–9
   school uniform *177*
   at Teen Choice Awards *64*
   100th episode *206*

Total Request Live 2007 112
   see also Serena Van Der Woodsen
locations
   budgets and 51–2
   deciding on 21–2
   early 34
Lonely Boy. *see* Dan Humphrey
Louis Grimaldi
   as annoying character 140
   Blair, relationship with 159
   lunacy/gravitas as missing in reboot 192

Manic Pixie Dream Girl, Serena as 133–7
marketing
   image for first season *35*
   OMFG campaign 44–6
   rumors about friendships between cast members 108–11
masturbation, female 129–30
McCall, Tyler 63, 72, 162, 204
Meester, Leighton 73
   after *Gossip Girl* 215
   casting as Blair 26–7

INDEX

fashion, *Gossip Girl* and 163–4
possibility of reboot, reaction to 190
Rolling Stone photoshoot 127–8
rumors about friendships between cast members 106–9
school uniform *177*
at Teen Choice Awards *64*
Total Request Live 2007 112
see also Blair Waldorf
meme-able moments 46–7
Go Piss Girl meme 112–13
menswear fashion 166–7
minors, age differential in sex and 123–4, 125–6
Momsen, Taylor
after *Gossip Girl* 217
casting as Jenny 24–5
exit of 49–51, *140*
fast-rise fame and 81–2
see also Jenny Humphrey
Morgenstein, Leslie 19
Mortimer, Tinsley 94
Musée D'Orsay, filming in 52
music, *Gossip Girl* and

"Believe" (The Bravery) 180
best moments 178–81
choice of 174–5
cost of 176
"Dark on Fire" (Turin Brakes) 181
importance of 174–5
"Signs" (Bloc Party) 180
"Sour Cherry" (The Kills) 179–80
"Starpower" (Sonic Youth) 180
"Tell Me A Lie" (Fratellis) 179
"The Ice Is Getting Thinner" (Death Cab for Cutie) 178
tone of the show and 176
"Whatcha Say" (Jason Derulo) 181
"Wild Wolves" (Athlete) 179
"With Me" (Sum 41) 178
"Young Folks" (Peter Bjorn and John) 178

Nate Archibald
in 2025 210
casting of Chace Crawford 27

INDEX

Catherine, relationship with 156–7
familial collapse/addict Dad storyline 65
Sage, relationship with 157
Vanessa, relationship with 157
Nelly Yuki
  reboot 100
  stereotyping of character 98–9
networks, television, before *Gossip Girl* 11–15
new/old money in reboot 194
New York, people of color in 95
The New Yorker, Dan's publication in 66–7
New York Magazine's Daily Intel blog 52–62
nostalgia, lack of in reboot 192–3
NYC Prep spinoff 196–201

O'Dell, Amy 170
old/new money in reboot 194
Olivia Burke, relationship with Dan 158–9

OMFG marketing campaign 44–6
100th episode *206*
online recaps and feedback 52–62
  see also fans
Oppenheim, Sebastian 198
Ostroff, Dawn 15, 19, 20, 42, 57, 170
outfits
  online feedback on *Gossip Girl* 58–9
  see also fashion, *Gossip Girl* and

Paolo, Connor, after *Gossip Girl* 218
paparazzi on set 76–8
parenting, lack of
  Jenny Humphrey and 123
  Lily Van Der Woodsen 104, 117, 119–21, 135
  Tomashoff, Kelli 200–1
Parents Television Council 130
Paris, France
  fans 85–7, *91*
  filming in 52
Patsavas, Alexandra 161, 174–5
perks of fame 84

INDEX

Pete Fairman 117, 124
Peterson, Peter Cary "PC" 199
pilot episode 8, 36–9
Piznarski, Mark 37, 38, 202
plotlines. *see* storylines
Poésy, Clémence 93
Ponzi scheme storyline 67
popularity, enduring, of *Gossip Girl* 202–7
predator, Pete as 124
pregnancy scare 122
Pressler, Jessica 47, 52–62, 149, 204–5

Queller, Jessica 60

Rabin, Nathan 133
Rapaport, David 22–3, 24, 25–6, 33–4
ratings 41–3
Reality Index 52–62
real-life spinoff *NYC Prep* 196–201
reboot
  actors in *191*
  announcement of 191–2
  campiness, lack of 193
  clothes 194

  diversity and 100–3
  flatness of, reasons for 192–5
  Kate Keller as Gossip Girl 195
  lunacy/gravitas as missing 192
  new/old money 194
  nostalgia, lack of 192–3
  possibility of, actors' reactions to 190
  social media interaction 193
recaps of *Gossip Girl* on Daily Intel blog 52–62
reception of *Gossip Girl* 41–3
relationships between actors 82–3
retail landscape, impact on 172–3
Robards, Sam
  casting as Howard "the Captain" Archibald 29–30
  fans on set and 74–5
Rolling Stone photoshoot 127–8
romantic pairings
  Blair and Chuck 141–55, *155*
  Blair and Louis 159

239

INDEX

Dan and Blair   156
Dan and Olivia   158–9
Jenny and Chuck   157–8
Nate and Catherine   156–7
Nate and Sage   157
Nate and Vanessa   157
Rufus and Ivy   158
Serena and Colin   158
Serena and Tripp   159
worst   156–9
see also sex on *Gossip Girl*
Roth, Peter   19
Rovzar, Chris   52–62, 103, 202
Rufus Humphrey
   in 2025   211–12
   Ivy, relationship with   158
rumors about friendships between
   cast members   106–10
Rutherford, Kelly
   after *Gossip Girl*   219
   casting as Lily Van Der
     Woodsen   31
   clothes, Lily's   166
   fans on set and   75
   possibility of reboot, reaction
     to   190
   social media in *Gossip
     Girl*   202

100th episode   *206*
   see also Lily Van Der Woodsen

Safran, Joshua   45, 48, 100,
   102–3, 105–6, 108,
   109–10, 149, 173, 191–2
Sage Spence
   as annoying character   140
   Nate, relationship with   157
Savage, Stephanie   8, 14, 19, 20,
   21–2, 30, 34, 43, 50, 51–2,
   56, 57, 59, 110, 111, 163,
   164, 165, 166, 169, 170,
   173, 174, 187, 189, 196
Schneider, Travis   172
school uniform   168, *177*
Schwartz, Josh   8, 15, 19–21,
   22, 23, 26, 30, 34, 43,
   50, 57, 110, 111, 174, 176,
   187–8, 189, 196
scripts, leaks of   80–1
secret sibling of Serena and Dan
   64–5
Secret Society storyline   65
security for actors   78
Serena Van Der Woodsen
   in 2025   207–8
   attitudes towards sex   117–19

INDEX

casting of Blake Lively 23–4
Colin, relationship with 158
fashion, *Gossip Girl* and 164–6
Lily as parent 104, 117, 119–21, 135
as Manic Pixie Dream Girl 133–7
Nate, sex scene with 116
older men, relationships with 120–1
parents 104, 117, 119–20, 135
pilot episode 37–8
relationships with male characters 136–7
secret sibling of Serena and Dan 64–5
sex on *Gossip Girl* 116, 117–21
slut-shaming 117
Tripp, relationship with 159
sets
  fans at 73–80
  paparazzi at 76–8
settings
  budgets and 51–2
  choice of 37

Settle, Matthew
  after *Gossip Girl* 218
  100th episode 206
sex on *Gossip Girl*
  age differential 123–4, 125–6
  attitudes in 2000s 127
  Blair 121–2
  as built in from the start 116
  Dan Humphrey 125–6
  deleted scenes 131
  Euphoria, comparison with 126–7
  female masturbation 129–30
  generations, attitudes of previous 115–16
  hypersexualized, Chuck as 124–5
  Jenny Humphrey 123
  off-screen 127–9
  predator, Pete as 124
  pregnancy scare 122
  Rolling Stone photoshoot 127–8
  Serena 117–21
  sexual assaults by Chuck 124

INDEX

threesome – Dan, Vanessa and Olivia 130–1
today's content, comparison with 126–7
viewed today 116–17
writing, then/now comparison 129
see also romantic pairings
Shawn, Wallace 190
"Signs" (Bloc Party) 180
slut-shaming
   Blair 122
   pregnancy scares 122
   Serena 117
Snow, Brittany 93
social media
   beginnings of 71–2
   Gossip Girl and 4–7, 202
   Reality Index 52–62
   reboot 193
softness of interpersonal relationships 49
Solomon, Stephanie 172
"Sour Cherry" (The Kills) 179–80
spinoff *NYC Prep* 196–201
spoilers, fans and 80

Stan, Sebastian
   casting as Carter Baizen 31
   fast-rise fame and 81, 83–4
   recognition of for *Gossip Girl* character 85
"Starpower" (Sonic Youth) 180
storylines
   best 63, 65, 66–9
   Chuck, Elle, and the Secret Society 65
   Chuck trading Blair for father's hotel 67
   Dan and Georgina's faux baby storyline 66
   Dan as Gossip Girl 68–9
   Dan's publication in *The New Yorker* 66–7
   before end of *Gossip Girl* 183–4
   familial collapse/addict Dad, Nate's 65
   Gossip Girl, Dan revealed as 68–9
   Lola and Ivy and Carol and Rufus 68
   Ponzi scheme 67

INDEX

secret sibling of Serena and Dan   64–5
worst   62–3, 64–5, 66, 67–9
streaming services, viewing figures and   41–3
Szadkowski, Zuzanna
  casting as Dorota   30
  on Dorota comforting Blair   49, 63, 189–90
  enduring popularity of *Gossip Girl*   205
  fans on sets and   74, 75–6
  first appearance of character   49
  on online commenters   57
  see also Dorota Kishlovsky
Szohr, Jessica
  after *Gossip Girl*   217–18
  casting as Vanessa   28
  celebrities wanting to meet cast members   85
  fans in actors' hang-out spots   79
  fast-rise fame and   81
  on perks of fame   84
  personal security   78
  see also Vanessa Abrams

Teen Choice Awards   64
teen dramas
  author's experience   1–4
  beginnings of   13–15
  diversity, lack of in   95–6
  enduring popularity of *Gossip Girl*   206–7
  television before *Gossip Girl*   11–15
"Tell Me A Lie" (Fratellis)   179
"The Ice Is Getting Thinner" (Death Cab for Cutie)   178
themes of *Gossip Girl*   49
The O.C.   196
time-shifted viewing, viewing figures and   41–3
tokenism re: diversity   96
Tomashoff, Kelli   198, 200–1
Trachtenberg, Michelle
  after *Gossip Girl*   217
  camera phones, lack of   84–5
  casting as Georgina Sparks 32
  personal security   78
  on rumors about cast members   108
  see also Georgina Sparks
Tripp Vanderbilt, Serena and   136–7, 159

INDEX

UPN 13, 14, 15

Vanessa Abrams
 in 2025 211
 as annoying character 139
 casting of Jessica Szohr 28
 Nate, relationship with 157
viewing numbers 41–3
viral marketability, *Gossip Girl* and 6–7
von Ziegesar, Cecily 16–18

walking tours to sets/actors' hang out spots 78–9
Wang, Vera 93
WB 13, 14, 15
wedding of Lily Van Der Woodsen 51–2
Weiss, Shari 71–2, 107–8, 153, 154, 186, 205
Westwick, Ed
 after *Gossip Girl* 216
 allegations against 151–2, 154
 casting as Chuck 25–6

 on Chuck clothes 166–7
 fans on sets and 74
 marriage to Amy Jackson 154
 media stories about 107
 on set *132*
 see also Chuck Bass
"Whatcha Say" (Jason Derulo) 181
"Wild Wolves" (Athlete) 179
William Van Der Woodsen 139
"With Me" (Sum 41) 178
women on the show, treatment of 106–11
 see also individual characters
writers' strike, 2007–2008 43, 71
writing characters 48–51

"Young Folks" (Peter Bjorn and John) 178

Zhang, Nan 98
Zoe, Rachel 92

About the Author

Lindsay Denninger is an award-winning writer, celebrity interviewer, two-time Jeopardy! contestant, and storyteller who magically turned a love for nostalgic pop culture into a job. When she's not writing, streaming, or serving as copy director for major global brands, you can find her looking for snacks, reading at least a book a week, finding typos in restaurant menus, and lurking online. She lives on Long Island with her husband and dog.